SUPER CHRISTMAS ACTIVITIES
for Kids

SUPER CHRISTMAS ACTIVITIES
for Kids

2-IN-1
INCLUDES WINTER FUN & JESUS IS BORN

BARBOUR **kidz**

A Division of Barbour Publishing

ISBN 978-1-64352-973-8

Puzzles created by Rebecca Currington, Diane Whisner, and Belinda Mooney in association with Snapdragon Group, Tulsa, Oklahoma, USA.

All scripture quotations, unless otherwise noted, are taken from the King James Version of the Bible.

Published by Barbour Publishing, Inc., 1810 Barbour Drive, Uhrichsville, Ohio 44683, www.barbourbooks.com

Our mission is to inspire the world with the life-changing message of the Bible.

ecpa Member of the
Evangelical Christian
Publishers Association

Printed in the United States of America.

000879 0821 CM

C_N YO_ _I_T_U_E IT?

THE PICTURES ARE YOUR CLUES. USE THE CIRCLED LETTERS TO
COMPLETE THE PUZZLE BELOW.

THEY WILL BE THE PARENTS OF JESUS. WHO ARE THEY?

◯ ◯ ◯ ◯ ◯ ◯ & ◯ ◯ ◯ ◯

FIND THE FOUR

COMPLETE THE PUZZLE BELOW BY CROSSING OUT EVERY LETTER THAT APPEARS AT LEAST FOUR TIMES. USE THE REMAINING LETTERS TO COMPLETE THE SENTENCE.

B	J	C	T	C	T	S	I	W	Y	N
N	X	O	W	C	P	D	X	H	L	Z
J		L	R	K	U	P	N	V	V	B
P	I	Q	D	W	B	K	G	E	I	J
D	Q	O	H		M	I	S	Z	R	Q
S	G	A	E	V	O	Q	L	K	F	U
G	U	S	P	F	J	N	F			T
Z	K	Z	E	H	W	X	F		C	D
E	V	L	U	H	B	G	T		O	X

MARY AND JOSEPH PLAN TO __ __ __ __ __ __.

DON'T LEAVE IT SCRAMBLED!

UNSCRAMBLE EACH WORD. THEN USE THE CIRCLED LETTERS TO COMPLETE THE PUZZLE BELOW... AND I HOPE IT DOESN'T HURT YOUR EYES!

"NI HET TXHSI OHNMT, DGO

__ ___ _____ _____,

TSNE ETH EALGN IAGBLER

____ ___ _____ _____

OT RZHTENAA, A ONWT NI

__ _____, _ ____ __

EALLGIE, OT A NGIIVR

_____, __ _ _____

PDGELDE OT EB DMRAIRE

_____ __ __ _____

OT A ANM DMNEA HJSEPO,

__ _ ___ _____ _____,

A NCETDEASDN FO DVDIA."'

_ _____ __ _____."

LUKE 1:26–27

WHO IS THIS VISITOR?

◯◯◯◯◯◯◯
_ _ _ _ _ _ _

9

WHERE ARE THOSE VOWELS?

YOU'RE GOING TO HAVE TO CONCENTRATE FOR THIS ONE! VOWELS ARE HIDDEN IN THE PICTURE BELOW. YOU WILL NEED THEM TO COMPLETE THE PUZZLE.

"TH_ _NG_L W_NT T_ H_R _ND S__D, 'GR__T_NGS, Y__ WH_ _R_ H_GHLY F_V_R_D! TH_ L_RD _S W_TH Y__.'"

LUKE 1:28

LETTER CLUES

TO DECODE THIS MESSAGE FROM GOD, YOU'LL NEED TO TAKE THE LETTER FROM EACH NUMBERED CLUE AND MATCH IT TO THE NUMBERED SPACE IN THE PUZZLE BELOW.

1. LOOK FOR THIS IN BOTH *RAFT* AND *HORSE*.

   _____

2. THIS ONE IS SEEN ONCE IN *RUG* AND TWICE IN *JUGGLE*.

   _____

3. THIS LETTER IS FOUND TWICE IN *NONE* AND *NUN*.

   _____

4. BEGINS THE WORD *HOT* AND ENDS THE WORD *TOUGH*.

   _____

5. BEGINS THE WORD *OPEN* AND FOUND SECOND IN *ROPE*.

   _____

6. THIS LETTER IS FOUND ONCE IN *YELLOW* AND *BABY*.

   _____

7. THIS LETTER CAN BE FOUND IN *WHEEL* AND *SWIM*.

   _____

8. CAN BE SEEN THREE TIMES IN *TATTLE* AND ONCE IN *TOY*.

   _____

9. *HOLY* HAS ONE BUT *HOLLY* HAS TWO.

   _____

10. THIS LETTER IS FOUND IN *GIRLS* BUT NOT *GIRL*.

   _____

"'YOU __ILL BE WITH C__ I __D AND __IVE BIRTH TO
        7   4   9   2

A S__N, AND __OU A__E __O GIVE HIM THE __AME
    5   6   1   8   3

JE__ US.'"
   10   LUKE 1:31

11

PICTURE CLUES

THE PICTURES ARE YOUR ONLY CLUES TO COMPLETING THIS CROSSWORD. THIS IS A BIT OF A BRAIN TEASER.

UP OR DOWN?

UNSCRAMBLE THE WORDS, THEN IT'S UP TO YOU TO FIND WHERE EACH WORD GOES. WE PUT A FEW LETTERS IN TO HELP.

DBE _____   LTEANBK _____

MLBA _____   YOLHL _____

OEKYND _____   TSRA _____

CWO _____   LBLE _____

FIND THE FOUR

COMPLETE THE PUZZLE BELOW BY CROSSING OUT EVERY LETTER THAT APPEARS AT LEAST FOUR TIMES. USE THE REMAINING LETTERS TO COMPLETE THE SENTENCE.

MARY FINDS OUT THAT HER COUSIN, ELIZABETH, WILL ALSO HAVE A __ __ __ __ __ .

TRAVELIN' RHYMES

THIS IS A GREAT GAME TO PLAY AS YOU TRAVEL. YOU'LL NEED SOMEONE TO PLAY IT WITH, THOUGH, LIKE YOUR BROTHER OR SISTER OR FRIENDS.

BELOW IS A LIST OF WORD PAIRS THAT RHYME WITH EACH OTHER. YOUR JOB IS TO CALL OUT THE WORDS AND HAVE THE PLAYERS COME UP WITH THE SILLIEST RHYMES. WRITE THE BEST ON THE SPACES BELOW.

HAIR, BEAR	TACK, BACK
JUICE, LOOSE	SMILE, TRIAL
RUN, BUN	BIKE, LIKE
ICE, TWICE	ARROW, SPARROW
BALL, HALL	DARK, PARK

_____

_____

_____

_____

_____

_____

_____

_____

PICTURE MAKER

YOU MAKE THE PICTURE. DRAW THE IMAGE FROM EACH FRAME AT THE TOP IN THE FRAME BELOW WITH THE MATCHING NUMBER.

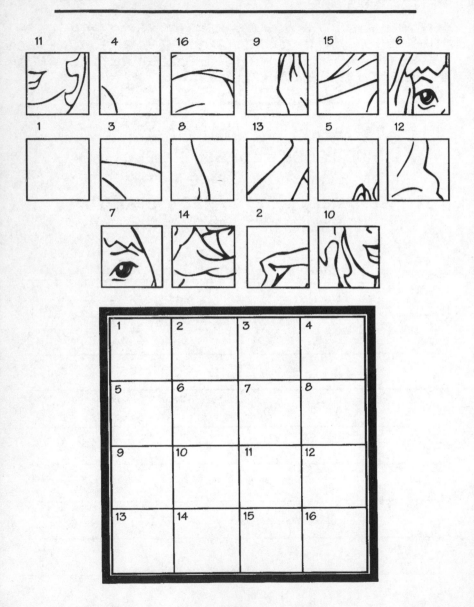

LET'S MAZE AROUND

MARY'S GOING TO VISIT HER COUSIN, ELIZABETH. CAN YOU HELP HER FIND HER WAY?

CAN YOU FIND THE WORDS?

ALL THESE WORDS ARE HIDDEN IN THE PUZZLE BELOW. HAVE FUN!

TREE
KING
MAGI
GALILEE
STAR

INN
JUDEA
CHILD
HEROD
CAMEL

```
            Y   J
            J   K
S D W K G F L R K F I W G P
T C H I L D H N U N D C
A A S H N B P W S G H A
X F R D T N B L D J B M
Q G D P S V H I O W V E
H N         L E F     N L
E W         J U S     C H
R B         G U L N B R P
O F         Y T D V I W I
D R         R T R E E G F
T D         R T H P A T D
Z F G A L I L E E M A O S M
```

18

WHERE ARE THOSE VOWELS?

YOU'RE GOING TO HAVE TO CONCENTRATE FOR THIS ONE! VOWELS ARE HIDDEN IN THE PICTURE BELOW. YOU WILL NEED THEM TO COMPLETE THE PUZZLE.

"WH _ N _ L _ Z _ B _ TH H _ _ _ RD
M _ RY'S GR _ _ _ T _ NG, TH _ B _ BY
L _ _ P _ D _ N H _ R W _ MB, _ ND
_ L _ Z _ B _ TH W _ S F _ LL _ D
W _ TH TH _ H _ LY SP _ R _ T."

LUKE 1:41

REALLY SILLY STORIES

YOU CAN PLAY THIS GAME BY YOURSELF, BUT IT'S A LOT MORE FUN TO PLAY WITH OTHERS.

ASK EACH PLAYER TO CALL OUT THE KIND OF WORD INDICATED IN EACH SPACE—A NOUN OR ADJECTIVE OR ADVERB, FOR EXAMPLE—AND PLACE THAT WORD IN THE APPROPRIATE SPACE. DO NOT TELL ANYONE WHAT THE STORY IS ABOUT—IT'S MORE FUN THAT WAY!

BELOW YOU'LL FIND A DESCRIPTION OF WHAT VERBS, NOUNS, ADJECTIVES, ADVERBS, ETC., ARE—JUST IN CASE YOU NEED A LITTLE HELP.

VERB: AN ACTION WORD, LIKE *WALK*, *RUN*, OR *FLY*. MAY BE *WALKED*, *RAN*, OR *FLEW*, IF <u>PAST TENSE</u> IS CALLED FOR.

ADVERB: MODIFIES A VERB AND USUALLY ENDS IN "LY." *SLOWLY* AND *CAREFULLY* ARE A COUPLE OF EXAMPLES.

NOUN: A PERSON, PLACE, OR THING, LIKE *BOY*, *BOAT*, OR *CAR*.

ADJECTIVE: DESCRIBES SOMEONE OR SOMETHING. *DIRTY*, *SILLY*, AND *BIG* ARE A FEW EXAMPLES.

PLACE: COULD BE A *COUNTRY* OR *CITY*, ETC.

PLURAL: MORE THAN ONE ITEM, SUCH AS *GIRLS* IS THE PLURAL OF *GIRL*.

NOW MOVE ON TO THE FOLLOWING PAGE TO PLAY THIS REALLY SILLY GAME!

REALLY SILLY STORIES

DON'T LOOK AT THE STORY BELOW. INSTEAD, FILL IN THE BLANKS IN THE LIST BELOW WITH THE REQUIRED WORDS. THEN FILL IN THE BLANKS IN THE STORY AND GET READY TO LAUGH UNCONTROLLABLY!

PLURAL NOUN _____
ADJECTIVE _____
ADJECTIVE _____
NAME _____
NOUN _____
VERB (PAST TENSE) _____
NOUN _____
ADJECTIVE _____
VERB ENDING IN "ING" _____
VERB (PAST TENSE) _____
ADJECTIVE _____
ADVERB _____

VERB (PAST TENSE) _____
NAME _____
VERB (PAST TENSE) _____
ADJECTIVE _____
VERB _____
NOUN _____
NAME OF SEASON _____
NOUN _____
VERB _____
VERB (PAST TENSE) _____
VERB (PAST TENSE) _____
NOUN _____

THE GRADE SIX _____ AT CENTRAL _____ SCHOOL
               PLURAL NOUN   ADJECTIVE

WERE LOOKING _____ TO THEIR TRIP TO _____
                 ADJECTIVE   NAME

MOUNTAIN. THE _____ HAD FINALLY _____ AND
                   NOUN   VERB (PAST TENSE)

_____ WAS _____ FOR _____. THEY _____
 NOUN   ADJECTIVE   VERB — "ING"   VERB (PAST TENSE)

ON SPENDING THE _____ DAY _____ AND ALL EAGERLY
                 ADJECTIVE   ADVERB

_____ THE FUN AHEAD. _____, HOWEVER, WAS
VERB (PAST TENSE)   NAME

_____ ABOUT _____ THING; WOULD HE STILL
VERB (PAST TENSE)   ADJECTIVE

_____ THE _____ TO PERFORM IN THE _____
 VERB   NOUN   NAME OF SEASON

PLAY AT HIS _____, LATER IN THE EVENING? HE DIDN'T
           NOUN

_____ TO MISS IT AND _____ HE HADN'T _____ ON
VERB   VERB (PAST TENSE)   VERB (PAST TENSE)

TOO MUCH FOR ONE _____.
              NOUN

DON'T LEAVE IT SCRAMBLED!

UNSCRAMBLE EACH WORD. THEN USE THE CIRCLED LETTERS TO COMPLETE THE PUZZLE BELOW... AND I HOPE IT DOESN'T HURT YOUR EYES!

"SCBEAEU SHEOJP RHE DSBHNUA

"_ O _ _ _ _   _ _ _ _ _ _   _ _ _   _ _ _ _ _ _ _

SWA A OGRIUHSTE ANM DAN

_ _ _   _   _ _ _ _ _ _ _ _   _ O _   _ _ _

IDD TNO TANW OT PSXOEE RHE

_ _ _   O _ _   _ _ _ _   _ _   _ _ O _ _ _   _ _ _

OT UCLPIB AIGERDSC, EH DHA NI

_ _   _ _ O _ _ _   _ _ _ _ _ _ _ _,   _ _   _ _ _   _ _

DMNI OT RVOECDI EHR YUQLITE."

_ _ _ _   _ _   _ _ O _ _ _ _   _ _ _   _ _ _ _ _ _."

MATTHEW 1:19

WHAT DID JOSEPH PLAN TO DO ABOUT THE WEDDING?

◯ ◯ ◯ ◯ ◯ ◯
_ _ _ _ _ _

22

it's a Mystery

THIS IS A GREAT GAME TO PLAY AS YOU TRAVEL. YOU'LL NEED SOMEONE TO PLAY IT WITH, THOUGH, LIKE YOUR BROTHER OR SISTER OR FRIENDS.

BELOW IS A LIST OF PHRASES THAT NEED TO BE COMPLETED. SHOW THIS PUZZLE TO EACH PLAYER, WHO PICKS A LETTER TO FILL IN THE BLANKS, AND THEN HAS TEN SECONDS TO GUESS THE PHRASE. MOVE ON TO EACH PLAYER UNTIL THE MYSTERY IS SOLVED! AS THE HOST OF THIS GAME, YOU GET TO CHECK OUT THE SOLUTION FROM THE ANSWER PAGES AT THE BACK (IF YOU NEED TO)!

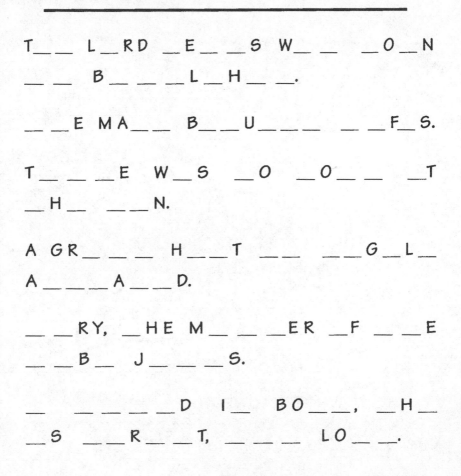

T _ _ L _ R D _ E _ _ S W _ _ _ O _ N
_ _ B _ _ _ L _ H _ _ .

_ _ E M A _ _ _ B _ _ U _ _ _ _ _ F _ S.

T _ _ _ E W _ S _ O _ O _ _ _ T
_ H _ _ _ N.

A G R _ _ _ _ H _ _ T _ _ _ _ G _ L _
A _ _ _ A _ _ D.

_ _ R Y, _ H E M _ _ _ _ E R _ F _ _ _ E
_ _ B _ J _ _ _ _ S.

_ _ _ _ _ _ D I _ B O _ _ _, _ H _
_ S _ _ R _ _ T, _ _ _ L O _ _ .

23

CAN YOU PICTURE IT?

THE PICTURES ARE YOUR CLUES. USE THE CIRCLED LETTERS TO COMPLETE THE PUZZLE BELOW.

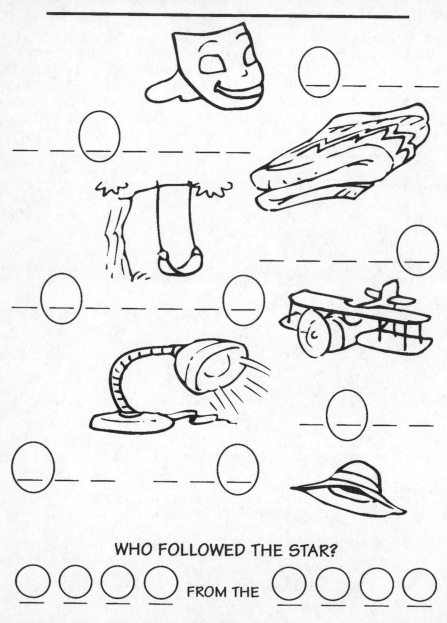

WHO FOLLOWED THE STAR?

◯ ◯ ◯ ◯ FROM THE ◯ ◯ ◯ ◯
___ ___ ___ ___   ___ ___ ___ ___

24

UP OR DOWN?

UNSCRAMBLE EACH WORDS.
THEN IT'S UP TO YOU TO FIND WHERE
EACH WORD GOES! WE PUT A FEW
LETTERS IN TO HELP.

HSJEPO _____   ATS _____
TTNE _____   NDE _____
RMREDIA _____   SJESU _____
TEBALS _____   SNO _____

WHAT CAN I SAY?
I *LOVE* THE WOMAN!

WHO, WHAT, WHERE

THIS IS A GREAT GAME TO PLAY AS YOU TRAVEL. YOU'LL NEED SOMEONE TO PLAY IT WITH, THOUGH, LIKE YOUR BROTHER OR SISTER OR FRIENDS.

BELOW IS A LIST OF QUESTIONS THAT NEED A "WHO, WHAT, OR WHERE" ANSWER. EACH PLAYER HAS TEN SECONDS TO ANSWER. AS THE HOST OF THIS GAME, YOU GET TO CHECK OUT THE SOLUTION FROM THE ANSWER PAGES AT THE BACK (IF YOU NEED TO)!

THIS YOUNG GIRL WAS VISITED BY AN ANGEL WITH GOOD NEWS. *WHO* WAS SHE? _____

LUKE 1:26–33

THIS RULER WAS VERY AFRAID OF THE BIRTH OF JESUS CHRIST. *WHO* WAS HE? _____

MATTHEW 2:3

MARY TRAVELED WITH JOSEPH TO THIS PROVINCE TO GIVE BIRTH. *WHERE* WERE THEY? _____

LUKE 2:4

THIS PLACE WAS FULL, FORCING THE YOUNG COUPLE TO GO ELSEWHERE. *WHAT* WAS IT? _____

LUKE 2:7

HAVING BEEN WARNED, JOSEPH TOOK HIS FAMILY HERE TO LIVE. *WHERE* ARE THEY? _____

MATTHEW 2:13–15

THIS LED MAGI FROM THE EAST TO THE BIRTHPLACE OF CHRIST. *WHAT* WAS IT? _____

MATTHEW 2:9

PICTURE CLUES

THE PICTURES ARE YOUR ONLY CLUES TO COMPLETING THIS CROSSWORD. THIS IS A BIT OF A BRAIN TEASER.

ALL JUMBLED UP

HEY . . . THIS ONE WILL BE FUN!
FIND THE OPPOSITE OF EACH WORD,
THEN USE THE CIRCLED LETTERS TO
COMPLETE THE PUZZLE BELOW.

MOTHER   _ _ _ _ O _

SUN   O _ _ _

PEN   _ O _ _ _ O

DOG   _ O _

DAY   _ _ _ O _

COLD   O _ _

STRAIGHT   O _ _ _

TIRED   _ _ _ _ O

WHERE DID THE MIRACLE BEGIN?

O O O O O O O O O
_ _ _ _ _ _ _ _ _

PICTURE MAKER

YOU MAKE THE PICTURE. DRAW THE IMAGE FROM EACH FRAME AT THE TOP IN THE FRAME BELOW WITH THE MATCHING NUMBER.

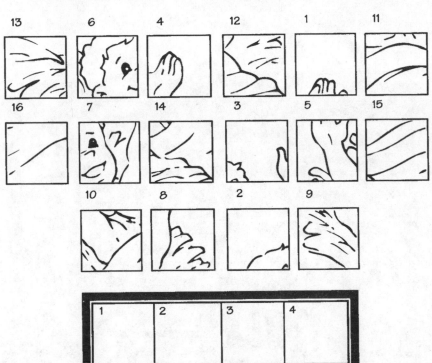

LET'S MAZE AROUND

WE ARE IN BETHLEHEM, AND MARY AND JOSEPH NEED HELP
FINDING A PLACE FOR HER TO GIVE BIRTH. CAN YOU HELP?

JUST A REGULAR OLD CROSSWORD!

ACROSS

1. HEAVENLY HOST
2. A SPECIAL BABY
3. PLACE FOR ANIMALS
4. CRIB FOR JESUS
5. RIDDEN BY MARY
6. A FALSE GOD

DOWN

1. JESUS' BIRTHPLACE
2. PROVINCE OF ISRAEL
3. THEY CARE FOR SHEEP
4. LARGE GROUP OF SHEEP
5. THE CREATOR
6. ANCIENT MOTEL

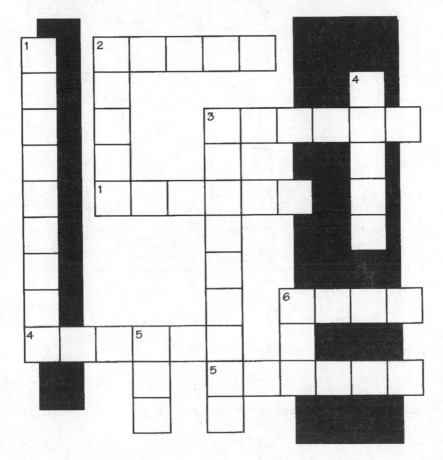

WHERE ARE THOSE VOWELS?

YOU'RE GOING TO HAVE TO CONCENTRATE FOR THIS ONE! VOWELS ARE HIDDEN IN THE PICTURE BELOW. YOU WILL NEED THEM TO COMPLETE THE PUZZLE.

"SH _ _   WR _ PP _ D   H _ M   _ N
CL _ THS   _ ND   PL _ C _ D   H _ M
_ N   _   M _ NG _ R,   B _ C _ _ S _
TH _ R _   W _ S   N _   R _ _ M
F _ R   TH _ M   _ N   TH _   _ NN."

LUKE 2:7

LETTER CLUES

TO DECODE THIS MESSAGE FROM GOD, YOU'LL NEED TO TAKE
THE LETTER FROM EACH NUMBERED CLUE AND MATCH IT TO
THE NUMBERED SPACE IN THE PUZZLE BELOW.

1. THIS LETTER BEGINS *HAIR* AND ENDS *ROUGH*.
   _____

2. FOUND SECOND TO LAST IN BOTH *LOVE* AND *LEAVE*.
   _____

3. FOUND ONCE IN *CRUMB* AND TWICE IN *ACCEPT*.
   _____

4. THIS ONE'S TWICE IN *EFFECT* BUT ONCE IN *FAIR*.
   _____

5. YOU'LL FIND THIS ONE IN *BEST* BUT NOT IN *BUST*.
   _____

6. YOU'LL FIND THIS TWICE IN *BABY* AND ONCE IN *BOAT*.
   _____

7. THIS LETTER BEGINS *GOAT* AND ENDS *JOG*.
   _____

"AND T _ _ R _   W _ R _   S _ _ P _ _ RDS
      1 5 5   5 5   1 5   1 5

LI _ IN _   OUT IN T _ _   _ I _ LDS N _ AR _ Y,
   2   7   1 5   4 5   5   6

K _ _ PIN _   WAT _ _   O _ _ R   T _ _ IR
  5 5   7   3 1   2 5   1 5

_ LO _ KS   AT   NI _ _ T."
4   3   7 1

LUKE 2:8

33

CAN YOU FIND THE WORDS?

ALL THESE WORDS ARE HIDDEN IN THE PUZZLE BELOW. *HAVE FUN!*

BASKET	JOSEPH
CHURCH	BIBLE
TEMPLE	STAR
SUNDAY	MANGER
FLOCK	MAGI

```
                B W
              S A T
              J S F U
              K Q K Z C V
  S T A R N B E S U N D A Y R
  G Y E S T R T Z M B K Y C H
      D L M P F P M T W S B N
      V H P J K J A L M I
      U N F L O C K N A B
      B C D Z L E S G Y G L
      P C H U R C H E Q I E
      W Q T J        P Z D R
  P H F                H R G
  M                      K U
```

FIND THE FOUR

COMPLETE THE PUZZLE BELOW BY CROSSING OUT EVERY LETTER THAT APPEARS AT LEAST FOUR TIMES. USE THE REMAINING LETTERS TO COMPLETE THE SENTENCE.

WELL . . . / COULD USE AN ANGEL RIGHT ABOUT NOW!

M	V	X	K	M	Q	W	R	I	Y
H	G	B	Z	S	C	C	K	E	X
R	P	J	B	F	Z	Q	V	H	R
C	T	Q	W	H		Z	C	D	K
U	K	D	J	U	I	J	S	V	T
W	O	M	Z	O	X	M	D	O	Y
S	N	U	P	Y	L	P	Y	B	F
F	P	X	O	D	R	T	F	Q	V
I	W	T	I	A	J	S	U	H	B

AN _ _ _ _ _ APPEARS TO THE SHEPHERDS.

UP OR DOWN?

UNSCRAMBLE THE WORDS. THEN IT'S UP TO YOU TO FIND WHERE EACH WORD GOES. WE PUT A FEW LETTERS IN TO HELP.

ISHHGTE _____   WCAHT _____

ONTW _____   SHTO _____

GYLRO _____   DLGA _____

VLNYEEAH _____   ISH _____

DLRO _____   AEHRT _____

HNEOS _____   ERATH _____

WHO, WHAT, WHERE

THIS IS A GREAT GAME TO PLAY AS YOU TRAVEL. YOU'LL NEED SOMEONE TO PLAY IT WITH, THOUGH, LIKE YOUR BROTHER OR SISTER OR FRIENDS.

BELOW IS A LIST OF QUESTIONS THAT NEED A "WHO, WHAT, OR WHERE" ANSWER. EACH PLAYER HAS TEN SECONDS TO ANSWER. AS THE HOST OF THIS GAME, YOU GET TO CHECK OUT THE SOLUTION FROM THE ANSWER PAGES AT THE BACK (IF YOU NEED TO)!

SHEPHERDS WERE AT WORK, LOOKING AFTER THEIR SHEEP. *WHERE* WERE THEY? _____

LUKE 2:8

SUDDENLY, SOMETHING SHONE ALL AROUND THEM. *WHAT* WAS IT? _____

LUKE 2:9

HE BROUGHT THEM GOOD NEWS OF GREAT JOY FOR ALL PEOPLE. *WHO* WAS HE? _____

LUKE 2:10

A SAVIOR HAD BEEN BORN WHO WAS CHRIST, THE LORD. *WHERE* WAS HE BORN? _____

LUKE 2:11

ALL GLORY WAS GIVEN TO HIM BY THE ANGELS AND ALL MEN. *WHO* WAS HE? _____

LUKE 2:14

HE HAD NO BED, BUT THEY FOUND A PLACE TO LAY HIM DOWN. *WHAT* WAS IT? _____

LUKE 2:12

PEACE WAS GIVEN TO THEM ON WHOM RESTED THE FAVOR OF GOD. *WHO* WERE THEY? _____

LUKE 2:14

PICTURE MAKER

YOU MAKE THE PICTURE. DRAW THE IMAGE FROM EACH FRAME AT THE TOP IN THE FRAME BELOW WITH THE MATCHING NUMBER.

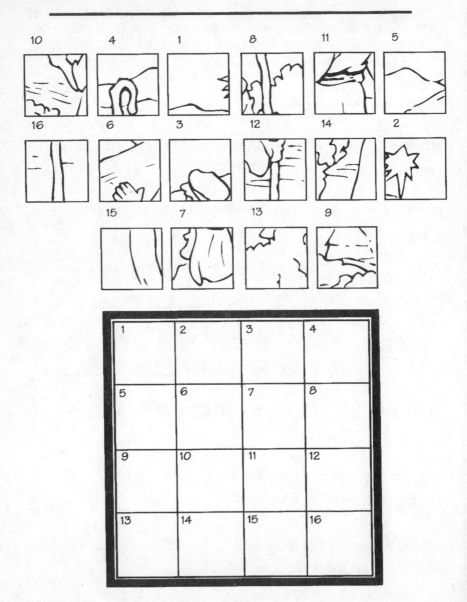

DON'T LEAVE IT SCRAMBLED!

UNSCRAMBLE EACH WORD. THEN USE THE CIRCLED LETTERS TO COMPLETE THE PUZZLE BELOW... AND I HOPE IT DOESN'T HURT YOUR EYES!

"LDSUYNDE   A   RTEAG   MCAYNOP   FO

" _ _ _ _ _ _ _   _   _○_ _ _ _   _ _ _ _ _ _ _   _ _

HET   VHNEEAYL   STHO   EEAARPDP   WHTI

_ _ _   _○_ _ _ _ _ _   _ _ _ _   _ _ _ _ _ _ _ _   _ _ _ _

ETH   NEALG,   IISPRGAN   DGO   NDA

_ _ _   _○_ _ _ _,   _ _ _ _ _ _ _ _   _ _ _   _ _ _

NASYGI,   'OGLRY   OT   ODG   NI   HET

_ _ _ _ _ _,   '_ _ _ _ _   _ _   _○_ _   _ _   _ _ _

EIHSTGH,   NAD   NO   TERAH   ECPEA

_ _○_ _ _ _,   _ _ _   _ _   _ _ _ _ _   _○_ _ _ _

OT   NME   NO   OWMH   ISH   AFRVO

_ _   _ _ _   _ _   _ _ _ _   _○_ _   _ _ _ _ _

TRSES.'"

_ _ _ _ _.'"

LUKE 2:13–14

THE HOST OF ANGELS

○ ○ ○ ○ ○ ○ ○   GOD.
_ _ _ _ _ _ _

39

REALLY SILLY STORIES

YOU *CAN* PLAY THIS *GAME* BY YOURSELF, BUT IT'S A LOT MORE FUN TO PLAY WITH OTHERS.

ASK EACH PLAYER TO CALL OUT THE KIND OF WORD INDICATED IN EACH SPACE—A NOUN OR ADJECTIVE OR ADVERB, FOR EXAMPLE—AND PLACE THAT WORD IN THE APPROPRIATE SPACE. DO NOT TELL ANYONE WHAT THE STORY IS ABOUT— IT'S MORE FUN THAT WAY!

BELOW YOU'LL FIND A DESCRIPTION OF WHAT VERBS, NOUNS, ADJECTIVES, ADVERBS, ETC., ARE—JUST IN CASE YOU NEED A LITTLE HELP.

<u>VERB</u>: AN ACTION WORD, LIKE *WALK, RUN,* OR *FLY.* MAY BE *WALKED, RAN,* OR *FLEW,* IF <u>PAST TENSE</u> IS CALLED FOR.

<u>ADVERB</u>: MODIFIES A VERB AND USUALLY ENDS IN "LY." *SLOWLY* AND *CAREFULLY* ARE A COUPLE OF EXAMPLES.

<u>NOUN</u>: A PERSON, PLACE, OR THING, LIKE *BOY, BOAT,* OR *CAR.*

<u>ADJECTIVE</u>: DESCRIBES SOMEONE OR SOME-THING. *DIRTY, SILLY,* AND *BIG* ARE A FEW EXAMPLES.

<u>PLACE</u>: COULD BE A *COUNTRY* OR *CITY,* ETC.

<u>PLURAL</u>: MORE THAN ONE ITEM, SUCH AS *GIRLS* IS THE PLURAL OF *GIRL.*

NOW MOVE ON TO THE FOLLOWING PAGE TO PLAY THIS REALLY SILLY GAME!

REALLY SILLY STORIES

DON'T LOOK AT THE STORY BELOW. INSTEAD, FILL IN THE BLANKS IN THE LIST BELOW WITH THE REQUIRED WORDS. THEN FILL IN THE BLANKS IN THE STORY AND GET READY TO LAUGH UNCONTROLLABLY!

PLURAL NOUN ———————   VERB ———————
NOUN ———————   ADVERB ———————
PLURAL NOUN ———————   NOUN ———————
VERB ———————   PLURAL NOUN ———————
NOUN ———————   NOUN ———————
NOUN ———————   NOUN ———————
ADJECTIVE ———————   VERB (PAST TENSE) ———————
PLURAL NOUN ———————   PLURAL NOUN ———————
VERB ENDING IN "ING" ———————   VERB ———————
TIME OF DAY ———————   NOUN ———————
PLURAL NOUN ———————   NOUN ———————
PLURAL NOUN ———————   VERB ENDING IN "ING" ———————
PLURAL NOUN ———————   ADJECTIVE ———————
VERB (PAST TENSE) ———————

THE _____ FROM THE SUNDAY _____ CLASS WERE
   PLURAL NOUN   NOUN

ALL IN THEIR _____ AND COULD HARDLY _____
        PLURAL NOUN   VERB

THEIR _____. THE _____ WAS ABOUT TO START!
     NOUN   PLURAL NOUN

FOR THE _____ TWO _____, THEY HAD BEEN
       ADJECTIVE   PLURAL NOUN

_____ FOR THIS SPECIAL _____, BUILDING
VERB—"ING"   TIME OF DAY

_____, SEWING _____, AND LEARNING THEIR
PLURAL NOUN   PLURAL NOUN

_____. THEY WERE _____ IN THEIR RESOLVE
PLURAL NOUN   VERB (PAST TENSE)

TO _____ THIS THE BEST PLAY ANYONE HAD _____
   VERB   ADVERB

SEEN. FINALLY, THE _____ ARRIVED. THE
                  NOUN

_____ DIMMED AND A _____ FELL OVER THE
PLURAL NOUN   NOUN

_____. THE CURTAIN _____ AND THE _____
NOUN   VERB (PAST TENSE)   PLURAL NOUN

WERE GRATIFIED TO _____ THE EXPRESSIONS OF
                VERB

_____ FROM EVERYONE IN THE _____. THIS WAS
NOUN   NOUN

_____ TO BE A _____ NIGHT!
VERB-"ING"   ADJECTIVE

41

JUST A REGULAR OLD CROSSWORD!

ACROSS

1. JESUS WAS BORN THERE
2. GIVE LIGHT
3. COMPANY OF ANGELS
4. TOWN OF _____
5. THE ANGELS WERE DOING IT

DOWN

1. BORN TO MARY
2. A CARPENTER
3. VERY HIGH
4. VERY AFRAID
5. HE WOULD BRING THIS

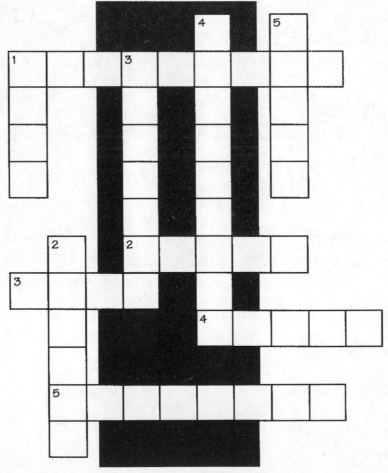

42

TRAVELIN' RHYMES

THIS IS A GREAT GAME TO PLAY AS YOU TRAVEL. YOU'LL NEED SOMEONE TO PLAY IT WITH, THOUGH, LIKE YOUR BROTHER OR SISTER OR FRIENDS.

BELOW IS A LIST OF WORD PAIRS THAT RHYME WITH EACH OTHER. YOUR JOB IS TO CALL OUT THE WORDS AND HAVE THE PLAYERS COME UP WITH THE SILLIEST RHYMES. WRITE THE BEST ON THE SPACES BELOW.

TRAVEL, GRAVEL   HEART, START
HOST, COAST   CLEANER, MEANER
SUN, FUN   CAR, STAR
CARE, FAIR   BLOW, GROW
BED, SLED   GREETING, MEETING

FIND THE FOUR

COMPLETE THE PUZZLE BELOW BY CROSSING OUT EVERY LETTER THAT APPEARS AT LEAST FOUR TIMES. USE THE REMAINING LETTERS TO COMPLETE THE SENTENCE.

H	E	A	M	B	S	G	P	H	C
C	K	P	J	G	N	F	L	T	J
I	H	R	Q	T	K	U	E	S	N
P	Q	V	K	I	U	B	Y	G	H
F	B	T	W	F	M	Q	V	W	X
J	■	■	Y	X	P	S	Y	A	T
M	X	A	E	Q	O	J	I	N	C
V	Y	X	G	U	W	K	C	U	F
A	W	V	I	M	D	B	E	N	S

AT THE TOP . . .
AT THE TOP!

JESUS IS OUR SAVIOR AND OUR __ __ __ __ .

44

UP OR DOWN?

UNSCRAMBLE THE WORDS.
THEN IT'S UP TO YOU TO FIND WHERE
EACH WORD GOES. WE PUT A FEW
LETTERS IN TO HELP.

OIRSHPW _____
RADME _____
RHRYM _____
RTMHEO _____
TOYRNCU _____
PPRHOTE _____

FOR YOU!

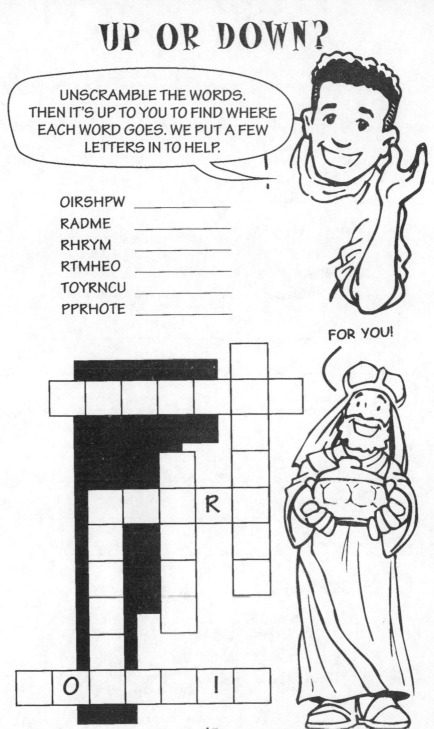

45

TRAVELIN' RHYMES

THIS IS A GREAT GAME TO PLAY AS YOU TRAVEL. YOU'LL NEED SOMEONE TO PLAY IT WITH, THOUGH, LIKE YOUR BROTHER OR SISTER OR FRIENDS.

BELOW IS A LIST OF WORD PAIRS THAT RHYME WITH EACH OTHER. YOUR JOB IS TO CALL OUT THE WORDS AND HAVE THE PLAYERS COME UP WITH THE SILLIEST RHYMES. WRITE THE BEST ON THE SPACES BELOW.

MIXTURE, FIXTURE   STRONG, LONG
SALT, MALT   GOOD, HOOD
LAW, SAW   SMILE, WHILE
FEAR, NEAR   STAR, FAR

_____

_____

_____

_____

_____

_____

_____

JUNE... SPOON...
LOON... DUNE...
MOON...

CAN YOU FIND THE WORDS?

ALL THESE WORDS ARE HIDDEN IN THE PUZZLE BELOW. HAVE FUN!

WARNED
DREAM
BOWED
KING
CHILD

MYRRH
TREASURE
GOLD
COUNTRY
REPORT

```
        W D W K
        T A F R
        L H R Z
N B K R F Z V M N E T S K B
G O T R E A S U R E A O I V
C W N E C N O H D F D M N K
J E G O L D R B H R B R G J
  D P L J R M T L O Y T E
  S S Z Y E J P W R G F A
    H M F A V A T E C H
    W D M R N M P B
      P G A U K B O D
      Z V N O E C O R L G
      R G K C H I L D T W P S
```

C A N   YO U   P I C T U R E   IT?

THE PICTURES ARE YOUR CLUES. USE THE CIRCLED LETTERS TO COMPLETE THE PUZZLE BELOW.

WHAT DID THE ANGEL TELL JOSEPH IN HIS DREAM?

◯ ◯   ◯ ◯   ◯ ◯ ◯ ◯ ◯

LET'S MAZE AROUND

HEROD WANTS TO FIND THE NEWBORN JESUS AND KILL HIM. HELP THE FAMILY ESCAPE TO EGYPT.

PICTURE MAKER

YOU MAKE THE PICTURE. DRAW THE IMAGE FROM EACH FRAME AT THE TOP IN THE FRAME BELOW WITH THE MATCHING NUMBER.

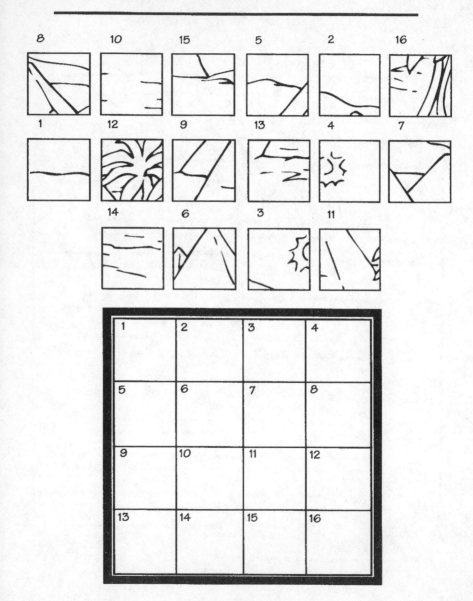

WHO, WHAT, WHERE

THIS IS A GREAT GAME TO PLAY AS YOU TRAVEL. YOU'LL NEED SOMEONE TO PLAY IT WITH, THOUGH, LIKE YOUR BROTHER OR SISTER OR FREINDS.

BELOW IS A LIST OF QUESTIONS THAT NEED A "WHO, WHAT, OR WHERE" ANSWER. EACH PLAYER HAS TEN SECONDS TO ANSWER. AS THE HOSE OF THIS GAME, YOU GET TO CHECK OUT THE SOLUTION FROM THE ANSWER PAGES AT THE BACK (IF YOU NEED TO)!

OH MY... GOTTA GO!

AN ANGEL TOLD THIS MAN, IN A DREAM, TO ESCAPE TO EGYPT. *WHO* WAS HE? _____

MATTHEW 2:13

THE FAMILY OF JESUS STAYED HERE UNTIL THE DEATH OF HEROD. *WHERE* WERE THEY? _____

MATTHEW 2:14–15

THEY MIGHT HAVE SEEN SOMETHING INCREDIBLE ON ARRIVAL. *WHAT* WAS IT? _____

FIND THE FOUR

COMPLETE THE PUZZLE BELOW BY CROSSING OUT EVERY LETTER THAT APPEARS AT LEAST FOUR TIMES. USE THE REMAINING LETTERS TO COMPLETE THE SENTENCE.

M	B	L	F	T	J	W	M	V	O
I	E	V	C	S	A	P	U	G	Q
K	T	W	N	Q	X	Y	N	X	J
L	G	J	Z	I	Z	L	■	A	Y
C	S	X	B	Z	F	Q	Z	C	B
P	N	R	Y	K	T	N	P	U	G
A	V	M	Q	F	S	G	Y	X	W
U	F	W	L	C	J	B	V	H	M
K	I	D	T	P	U	A	I	K	S

AFTER THE DEATH OF _ _ _ _ _ , THE FAMILY OF JESUS RETURNED TO NAZARETH.

PICTURE MAKER

YOU MAKE THE PICTURE. DRAW THE IMAGE FROM EACH FRAME AT THE TOP IN THE FRAME BELOW WITH THE MATCHING NUMBER.

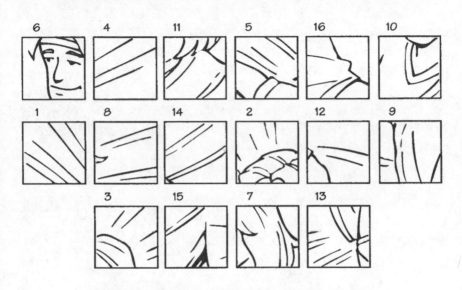

REALLY SILLY STORIES

YOU CAN PLAY THIS GAME BY YOURSELF, BUT IT'S A LOT MORE FUN TO PLAY WITH OTHERS.

ASK EACH PLAYER TO CALL OUT THE KIND OF WORD INDICATED IN EACH SPACE—A NOUN OR ADJECTIVE OR ADVERB, FOR EXAMPLE—AND PLACE THAT WORD IN THE APPROPRIATE SPACE. DO NOT TELL ANYONE WHAT THE STORY IS ABOUT— IT'S MORE FUN THAT WAY!

BELOW YOU'LL FIND A DESCRIPTION OF WHAT VERBS, NOUNS, ADJECTIVES, ADVERBS, ETC., ARE—JUST IN CASE YOU NEED A LITTLE HELP.

<u>VERB:</u> AN ACTION WORD, LIKE *WALK, RUN,* OR *FLY.* MAY BE *WALKED, RAN, OR FLEW,* IF <u>PAST TENSE</u> IS CALLED FOR.

<u>ADVERB:</u> MODIFIES A VERB AND USUALLY ENDS IN "LY." *SLOWLY* AND *CAREFULLY* ARE A COUPLE OF EXAMPLES.

<u>NOUN:</u> A PERSON, PLACE, OR THING, LIKE *BOY, BOAT,* OR *CAR.*

<u>ADJECTIVE:</u> DESCRIBES SOMEONE OR SOME-THING. *DIRTY, SILLY,* AND *BIG* ARE A FEW EXAMPLES.

<u>PLACE:</u> COULD BE A *COUNTRY* OR *CITY,* ETC.

<u>PLURAL:</u> MORE THAN ONE ITEM, SUCH AS *GIRLS* IS THE PLURAL OF *GIRL.*

NOW MOVE ON TO THE FOLLOWING PAGE TO PLAY THIS REALLY SILLY GAME!

REALLY SILLY STORIES

DON'T LOOK AT THE STORY BELOW. INSTEAD, FILL IN THE BLANKS IN THE LIST BELOW WITH THE REQUIRED WORDS. THEN FILL IN THE BLANKS IN THE STORY AND GET READY TO LAUGH UNCONTROLLABLY!

PLACE _____
ADJECTIVE _____
VERB (PAST TENSE) _____
ADJECTIVE _____
NOUN _____
PLURAL NOUN _____
ADVERB _____
VERB ENDING IN "ING" _____
NOUN _____
PART OF BUILDING _____
PLURAL NOUN _____
ADJECTIVE _____

VERB _____
ADJECTIVE _____
NOUN _____
PLURAL NOUN _____
NOUN _____
ADJECTIVE _____
NOUN _____
PLURAL NOUN _____
VERB (PAST TENSE) _____
PLURAL NOUN _____
NOUN _____
NAME OF SEASON _____

THE CHRISTMAS PLAY AT _____ WAS A _____ HIT!
                               PLACE   ADJECTIVE

WHY, THEY EVEN _____ A _____ _____ AND
                VERB (PAST TENSE)   ADJECTIVE   NOUN

ALL THE PARENTS AND _____ WERE FULL OF PRAISE
                           PLURAL NOUN

_____. NOW, ALL THE CHILDREN WERE _____
  ADVERB   VERB—"ING"

FORWARD TO THE _____ IN THE MAIN _____. THERE
              NOUN   PART OF BLDG.

WERE _____ FULL OF ALL KINDS OF _____ THINGS TO
      PLURAL NOUN   ADJECTIVE

_____ AND A WHOLE _____ _____ ENTIRELY FOR
VERB   ADJECTIVE   NOUN

_____. IT WAS STILL EARLY IN THE _____
PLURAL NOUN   NOUN

AND THE KIDS WERE _____ WITH GREAT ANTICIPATION
                   ADJECTIVE

FOR THE _____ WHEN THEY WERE TO GIVE THE _____
       NOUN   PLURAL NOUN

THEY HAD _____ ON FOR WEEKS, TO THEIR _____.
      VERB (PAST TENSE)   PLURAL NOUN

AFTER ALL, AS THEY HAD LEARNED IN THE _____, GIVING
                                      NOUN

WAS WHAT _____ WAS ALL ABOUT.
        NAME OF SEASON

JESUS IS BORN

DON'T LEAVE IT SCRAMBLED!

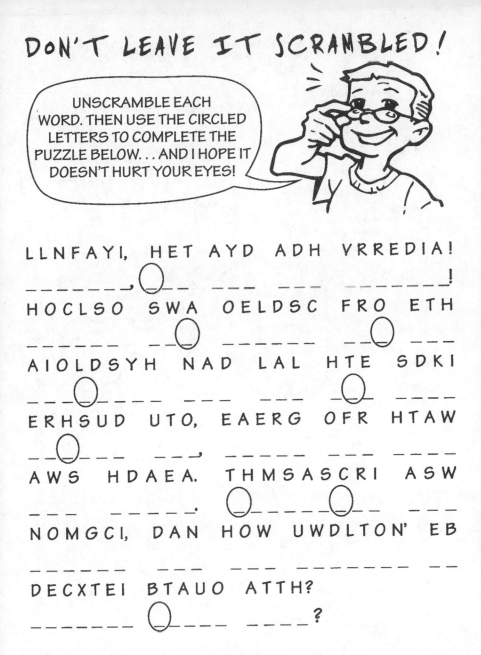

UNSCRAMBLE EACH WORD. THEN USE THE CIRCLED LETTERS TO COMPLETE THE PUZZLE BELOW... AND I HOPE IT DOESN'T HURT YOUR EYES!

LLNFAYI, HET AYD ADH VRREDIA!

_____, O__ ___ ___ _____!

HOCLSO SWA OELDSC FRO ETH

_____ ___ _____ __O___

AIOLDSYH NAD LAL HTE SDKI

_O_____ ___ ___ ___ ____

ERHSUD UTO, EAERG OFR HTAW

_O___ ___, _____ ___ ____

AWS HDAEA. THMSASCRI ASW

___ _____. __O__O___ ___

NOMGCI, DAN HOW UWDLTON' EB

_____ ___ ___ _____ __

DECXTEI BTAUO ATTH?

___O___ _____ ____?

IT'LL BE

O O O O O O O O O SOON!

WHERE ARE THOSE VOWELS?

YOU'RE GOING TO HAVE TO CONCENTRATE FOR THIS ONE! VOWELS ARE HIDDEN IN THE PICTURE BELOW. YOU WILL NEED THEM TO COMPLETE THE PUZZLE.

SCH_ _ _L'S _ _ _T F_ _R CHR_ _ST-M_ _S, _ND TH_ H_L_D_YS H_V_ B_G_N!

TRAVELIN' RHYMES

THIS IS A GREAT GAME TO PLAY AS YOU TRAVEL. YOU'LL NEED SOMEONE TO PLAY IT WITH, THOUGH, LIKE YOUR BROTHER OR SISTER OR FRIENDS.

BELOW IS A LIST OF WORD PAIRS THAT RHYME WITH EACH OTHER. YOUR JOB IS TO CALL OUT THE WORDS AND HAVE THE PLAYERS COME UP WITH THE SILLIEST RHYMES. WRITE THE BEST ON THE SPACES BELOW.

SNOW, GROW PLAY, GRAY
BALL, HALL SLED, FED
TREE, KNEE GREEN, SCREEN
EAT, FEET SKI, BEE

_____

_____

_____

_____

_____

_____

_____

it's a MYSTERY

THIS IS A GREAT GAME TO PLAY AS YOU TRAVEL. YOU'LL NEED SOMEONE TO PLAY IT WITH, THOUGH, LIKE YOUR BROTHER OR SISTER OR FRIENDS.

BELOW IS A LIST OF PHRASES THAT NEED TO BE COMPLETED. SHOW THIS PUZZLE TO EACH PLAYER, WHO PICKS A LETTER TO FILL IN THE BLANKS, AND THEN HAS TEN SECONDS TO GUESS THE PHRASE. MOVE ON TO EACH PLAYER UNTIL THE MYSTERY IS SOLVED! AS THE HOST OF THIS GAME, YOU GET TO CHECK OUT THE SOLUTION FROM THE ANSWER PAGES AT THE BACK (IF YOU NEED TO)!

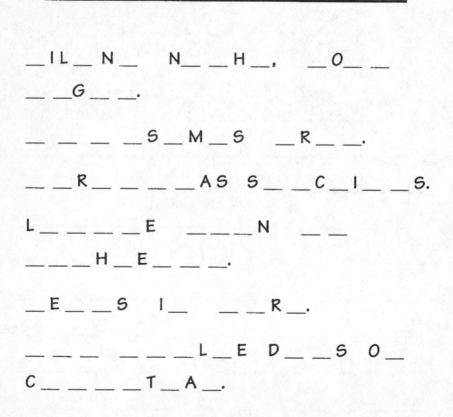

_ I L _ N _   N _ _ H _,   _ O _ _

_ _ G _ _.

_ _ _ _ S _ M _ S   _ R _ _.

_ _ R _ _ _ _ A S   S _ _ C _ I _ _ S.

L _ _ _ _ E   _ _ _ N   _ _

_ _ _ H _ E _ _ _.

_ E _ _ S   I _   _ _ R _.

_ _ _   _ _ _ _ L _ E   D _ _ S   O _

C _ _ _ _ T _ A _.

REALLY SILLY STORIES

YOU CAN PLAY THIS GAME BY YOURSELF, BUT IT'S A LOT MORE FUN TO PLAY WITH OTHERS.

ASK EACH PLAYER TO CALL OUT THE KIND OF WORD INDICATED IN EACH SPACE—A NOUN OR ADJECTIVE OR ADVERB, FOR EXAMPLE—AND PLACE THAT WORD IN THE APPROPRIATE SPACE. DO NOT TELL ANYONE WHAT THE STORY IS ABOUT—IT'S MORE FUN THAT WAY!

BELOW YOU'LL FIND A DESCRIPTION OF WHAT VERBS, NOUNS, ADJECTIVES, ADVERBS, ETC., ARE—JUST IN CASE YOU NEED A LITTLE HELP.

<u>VERB:</u> AN ACTION WORD, LIKE *WALK, RUN,* OR *FLY.* MAY BE *WALKED, RAN,* OR *FLEW,* IF <u>PAST TENSE</u> IS CALLED FOR.

<u>ADVERB:</u> MODIFIES A VERB AND USUALLY ENDS IN "LY." *SLOWLY* AND *CAREFULLY* ARE A COUPLE OF EXAMPLES.

<u>NOUN:</u> A PERSON, PLACE, OR THING, LIKE *BOY, BOAT,* OR *CAR.*

<u>ADJECTIVE:</u> DESCRIBES SOMEONE OR SOMETHING. *DIRTY, SILLY,* AND *BIG* ARE A FEW EXAMPLES.

<u>PLACE:</u> COULD BE A *COUNTRY* OR *CITY,* ETC.

<u>PLURAL:</u> MORE THAN ONE ITEM, SUCH AS *GIRLS* IS THE PLURAL OF *GIRL.*

NOW MOVE ON TO THE FOLLOWING PAGE TO PLAY THIS REALLY SILLY GAME!

REALLY SILLY STORIES

DON'T LOOK AT THE STORY BELOW. INSTEAD, FILL IN THE BLANKS IN THE LIST BELOW WITH THE REQUIRED WORDS. THEN FILL IN THE BLANKS IN THE STORY AND GET READY TO LAUGH UNCONTROLLABLY!

VERB—PAST TENSE _____
NOUN _____
NOUN _____
NOUN _____
NOUN _____
VERB _____
NOUN _____
NOUN _____
ADJECTIVE _____
NOUN _____
NOUN _____
TIME OF DAY _____

ADJECTIVE _____
NAME OF SEASON _____
NOUN _____
VERB—PAST TENSE _____
PLURAL NOUN _____
ADVERB _____
NOUN _____
NOUN _____
VERB—PAST TENSE _____
NOUN _____
VERB _____

WAYNE _____ ALL THE WAY _____ FROM SCHOOL. _____
    VERB (PAST TENSE)   NOUN   NOUN
WAS THE FIRST _____ OF THE _____ HOLIDAY AND HE
              NOUN   NOUN
COULD HARDLY _____ TO GET _____ AND PREPARE FOR THE
              VERB   NOUN
_____ THAT WAS _____. HE HEARD LAST _____ THAT IT
NOUN   ADJECTIVE   NOUN
WAS EVEN SUPPOSED TO _____ LATER IN THE
                       NOUN
_____! NOW, WASN'T THAT JUST _____? HE HAD
TIME OF DAY   ADJECTIVE
ALL HIS _____ GEAR TO GET OUT OF _____ AND
     NAME OF SEASON   NOUN
GET READY; HE _____ TO BE READY WHEN THE _____
         VERB (PAST TENSE)   PLURAL NOUN
WERE _____ WITH THAT WONDERFUL _____ STUFF. HE
   ADVERB   NOUN
NEEDED TO HAVE HIS _____ AND SKIS AND SNOW-
             NOUN
BOARD _____ AND WAXED AND READY FOR _____.
VERB (PAST TENSE)   NOUN
HOW WOULD HE EVER BE ABLE TO _____ TONIGHT?
                      VERB

CAN YOU FIND THE WORDS?

ALL THESE WORDS ARE HIDDEN IN THE PUZZLE BELOW. HAVE FUN!

SHARE
NATIVITY
BETHLEHEM
SHEPHERD
GOD
MARY

MAGI
ANGELS
CHURCH
JOSEPH
GIVE
CHRISTMAS

```
        C A
        V N
    B J M Q G L Y S
  W E W O T E O B K N
  D J T N M G L Z D O M S
K S O H V A C S G V S T H R
E T S L B R T J L M F U A T
J M E E T Y U I U A L E R F
Z P P H P L C G V G V G E H
T S H E P H E R D I J P Z J
T G O M J R Z U G F T G B L
  C H R I S T M A S C Y M
  F W T B O V M W S G
    C H U R C H S P
```

PICTURE MAKER

YOU MAKE THE PICTURE. DRAW THE IMAGE FROM EACH FRAME AT THE TOP IN THE FRAME BELOW WITH THE MATCHING NUMBER.

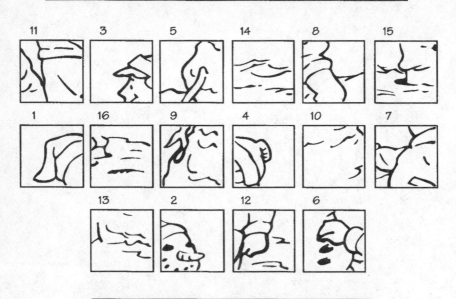

LET'S MAZE AROUND

SCHOOL'S OUT! HELP THE GANG GET HOME.

LESS SHALL BE FIRST

PLACE THE WORDS BELOW INTO THE PUZZLE ACCORDING TO THE NUMBER OF LETTERS IN EACH WORD, BEGINNING WITH THE WORD THAT HAS THE FEWEST LETTERS. THEN UNSCRAMBLE THE CIRCLED LETTERS TO COMPLETE THE ANSWER BELOW.

SNOWMAN   INSTRUCTOR
SPOON   PLAY
SHEPHERD   SCHOOL
GOD   CHRISTMAS

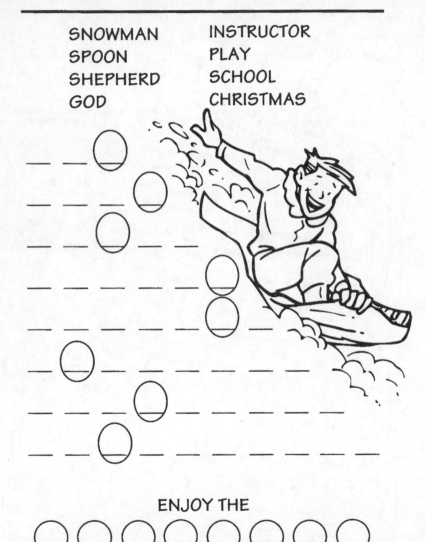

ENJOY THE

◯ ◯ ◯ ◯ ◯ ◯ ◯ ◯
_ _ _ _ _ _ _ _

68

WHO, WHAT, WHERE

THIS IS A GREAT GAME TO PLAY AS YOU TRAVEL. YOU'LL NEED SOMEONE TO PLAY IT WITH, THOUGH, LIKE YOUR BROTHER OR SISTER OR FRIENDS.

BELOW IS A LIST OF QUESTIONS THAT NEED A "WHO, WHAT, OR WHERE" ANSWER. EACH PLAYER HAS TEN SECONDS TO ANSWER. AS THE HOST OF THIS GAME, YOU GET TO CHECK OUT THE SOLUTION FROM THE ANSWER PAGES AT THE BACK (IF YOU NEED TO)!

THIS MAN HAS A LOT TO TEACH YOU IF YOU SHOW UP ONCE A WEEK. *WHO* IS HE? _____

HE'LL SHOW YOU HOW TO GET DOWN THE MOUNTAIN SAFELY. *WHO* IS HE? _____

IT DOESN'T FLY, AND IT MAKES YOUR MOUTH WATER EVERY YEAR. *WHAT* IS IT? _____

IT IS VERY DIFFICULT WAITING TO FIND OUT THE CONTENTS OF THIS. *WHAT* IS IT? _____

AT THIS TIME OF YEAR, YOU'RE THINKING OF WHAT IS AHEAD . *WHERE* ARE YOU?

_____

COMPLETE THE PUZZLE BELOW BY CROSSING OUT EVERY LETTER THAT APPEARS AT LEAST FOUR TIMES. USE THE REMAINING LETTERS TO COMPLETE THE SENTENCE.

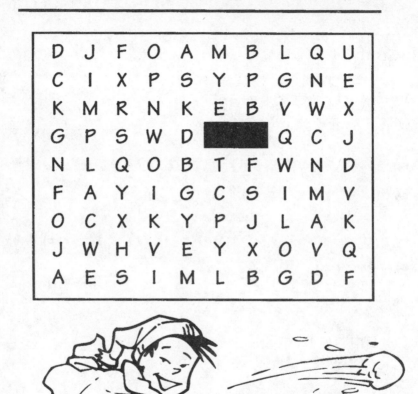

```
D  J  F  O  A  M  B  L  Q  U
C  I  X  P  S  Y  P  G  N  E
K  M  R  N  K  E  B  V  W  X
G  P  S  W  D  ██ ██ Q  C  J
N  L  Q  O  B  T  F  W  N  D
F  A  Y  I  G  C  S  I  M  V
O  C  X  K  Y  P  J  L  A  K
J  W  H  V  E  Y  X  O  V  Q
A  E  S  I  M  L  B  G  D  F
```

SNOWBALL FIGHTS ARE A LOT OF FUN, BUT TRY

NOT TO __ __ __ __ ANYONE!

TRAVELLIN' RHYMES

THIS IS A GREAT GAME TO PLAY AS YOU TRAVEL. YOU'LL NEED SOMEONE TO PLAY IT WITH, THOUGH, LIKE YOUR BROTHER OR SISTER OR FRIENDS.

BELOW IS A LIST OF WORD PAIRS THAT RHYME WITH EACH OTHER. YOUR JOB IS TO CALL OUT THE WORDS AND HAVE THE PLAYERS COME UP WITH THE SILLIEST RHYMES. WRITE THE BEST ON THE SPACES BELOW.

BOOK, HOOK	LIVE, GIVE
EGG, BEG	SLEIGH, TRAY
CANDY, HANDY	ICE, MICE
SCHOOL, COOL	PLAY, STAY
FLAKE, RAKE	BAND, HAND

_____

_____

_____

_____

_____

_____

_____

_____

JUST A REGULAR OLD CROSSWORD!

ACROSS

1. MUSIC PERFORMANCES
2. SNOW _____
3. FIRE BURNS IT
4. JUST LIKE SURFING
5. SEASONS MEANING
6. FISH THROUGH IT

DOWN

1. _____ HOLIDAY
2. SPECIAL SONGS
3. TEACHES ON MOUNTAIN
4. SKI _____
5. A SMALL TWIG
6. GOOD IN CABBAGE ROLLS

UP OR DOWN?

UNSCRAMBLE THE WORDS. THEN IT'S UP TO YOU TO FIND WHERE EACH WORD GOES. WE PUT A FEW LETTERS IN TO HELP.

ERTE _____

KURTYE _____

ENRTANSOM _____

NSRTEPE _____

HHBETELME _____

IANSGTK _____

A LITTLE FARTHER . . . AND YOU ARE MINE!

LETTER CLUES

TO DECODE THIS MESSAGE FROM *GOD*, YOU'LL NEED TO TAKE THE LETTER FROM EACH NUMBERED CLUE AND MATCH IT TO THE NUMBERED SPACE IN THE PUZZLE BELOW.

---

1. BEGINS THE WORD *NUT* AND ENDS THE WORD *MOON*.

   _____

2. APPEARS ONCE IN *ICE* AND TWICE IN *SKIING*.

   _____

3. THIS LETTER IS FOUND IN *BEGAN* BUT NOT IN *BEGUN*.

   _____

4. APPEARS TWICE IN *BOOT* BUT ONLY ONCE IN *POLE*.

   _____

5. FOUND TWICE IN BOTH *SNOWSHOE* AND *SOCKS*.

   _____

6. YOU'LL FIND THIS IN *LESS* BUT NOT IN *LOSS*.

   _____

7. BEGINS *TREE* AND IS IN THE MIDDLE OF *MOTOR*.

   _____

8. APPEARS ONCE IN *SISTER* AND TWICE IN *BROTHER*.

   _____

"Y_U W_LL B_ W_ _H CH_LD _ _D
   4   2   6   2 7   2   3 1

G_V_ B_ _ _H _ _ _ _ _ _, _ _D
  2 6   2 8 7   7 4 3 5 4 1   3 1

Y_U _ _ _ _ _ G_V_ H_M _H_
  4   3 8 6   7 4   2 6   2   7 6

_ _M_ J_ _U_."
1 3 6   6 5 5

LUKE 1:31

74

ALL JUMBLED UP

HEY . . . THIS ONE WILL BE FUN! FIND THE OPPOSITE OF EACH WORD, THEN USE THE CIRCLED LETTERS TO COMPLETE THE PUZZLE BELOW.

SNOW _ _ _ _ ◯

UP _ _ _ ◯

RECEIVE ◯ _ _ _

DARK _ ◯ _ _ _

FULL _ ◯ _ _ _

HAPPY _ ◯ _

SISTER _ _ _ _ _ ◯ _

CHRIST. THE TRUE

◯ ◯ ◯ ◯ ◯ ◯ ◯
_ _ _ _ _ _ _

OF CHRISTMAS.

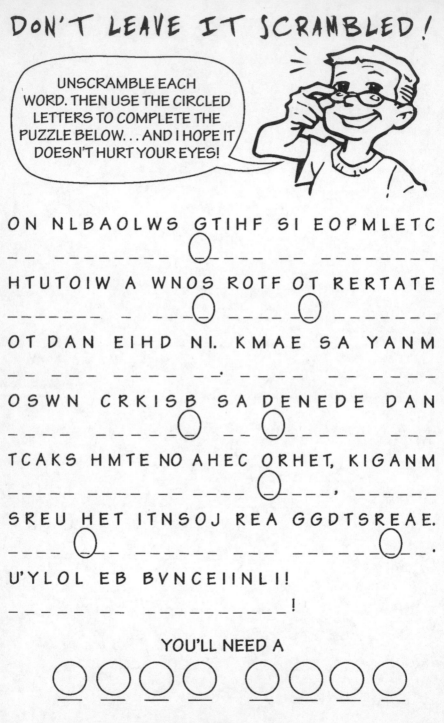

DON'T LEAVE IT SCRAMBLED!

UNSCRAMBLE EACH WORD. THEN USE THE CIRCLED LETTERS TO COMPLETE THE PUZZLE BELOW... AND I HOPE IT DOESN'T HURT YOUR EYES!

ON NLBAOLWS GTIHF SI EOPMLETC

__ _____ _____ __ _____

HTUTOIW A WNOS ROTF OT RERTATE

_____ _ ____ ____ __ _____

OT DAN EIHD NI. KMAE SA YANM

__ ___ ____ __. ____ __ ____

OSWN CRKISB SA DENEDE DAN

___ _____ __ _____ ___

TCAKS HMTE NO AHEC ORHET, KIGANM

_____ ____ __ ____ _____, _____

SREU HET ITNSOJ REA GGDTSREAE.

____ ___ _____ ___ _____.

U'YLOL EB BVNCEIINLI!

_____ __ _____!

YOU'LL NEED A

◯ ◯ ◯ ◯ ◯ ◯ ◯ ◯

REALLY SILLY STORIES

YOU CAN PLAY THIS GAME BY YOURSELF, BUT IT'S A LOT MORE FUN TO PLAY WITH OTHERS.

ASK EACH PLAYER TO CALL OUT THE KIND OF WORD INDICATED IN EACH SPACE—A NOUN OR ADJECTIVE OR ADVERB, FOR EXAMPLE—AND PLACE THAT WORD IN THE APPROPRIATE SPACE. DO NOT TELL ANYONE WHAT THE STORY IS ABOUT— IT'S MORE FUN THAT WAY!

BELOW YOU'LL FIND A DESCRIPTION OF WHAT VERBS, NOUNS, ADJECTIVES, ADVERBS, ETC., ARE—JUST IN CASE YOU NEED A LITTLE HELP.

<u>VERB</u>: AN ACTION WORD, LIKE *WALK*, *RUN*, OR *FLY*. MAY BE *WALKED*, *RAN*, OR *FLEW*, IF <u>PAST TENSE</u> IS CALLED FOR.

<u>ADVERB</u>: MODIFIES A VERB AND USUALLY ENDS IN "LY." *SLOWLY* AND *CAREFULLY* ARE A COUPLE OF EXAMPLES.

<u>NOUN</u>: A PERSON, PLACE, OR THING, LIKE *BOY*, *BOAT*, OR *CAR*.

<u>ADJECTIVE</u>: DESCRIBES SOMEONE OR SOME-THING. *DIRTY*, *SILLY*, AND *BIG* ARE A FEW EXAMPLES.

<u>PLACE</u>: COULD BE A *COUNTRY* OR *CITY*, ETC.

<u>PLURAL</u>: MORE THAN ONE ITEM, SUCH AS *GIRLS* IS THE PLURAL OF *GIRL*.

NOW MOVE ON TO THE FOLLOWING PAGE TO PLAY THIS REALLY SILLY GAME!

REALLY SILLY STORIES

DON'T LOOK AT THE STORY BELOW. INSTEAD, FILL IN THE BLANKS IN THE LIST BELOW WITH THE REQUIRED WORDS. THEN FILL IN THE BLANKS IN THE STORY AND GET READY TO LAUGH UNCONTROLLABLY!

_____

VERB _____

NOUN _____

ADVERB _____

NOUN _____

ADJECTIVE _____

ADJECTIVE _____

NOUN _____

PLURAL NOUN _____

VERB—PAST TENSE _____

NOUN _____

ADJECTIVE _____

VERB _____

PLURAL NOUN _____

ADJECTIVE _____

NOUN _____

NOUN _____

NOUN _____

VERB (ENDING IN "ING")

_____

NOUN _____

VERB (ENDING IN "ING")

_____

NOUN _____

ADJECTIVE _____

NOUN _____

FINALLY, THEY _____ AT THE TOP OF THE _____. THE DAY
      VERB   NOUN

_____ WAS FULL OF _____, WITH THE _____ OF
ADVERB   NOUN   ADJECTIVE

_____ RUNS DOWN FRESH _____. THEIR _____
ADJECTIVE   NOUN   PLURAL NOUN

WERE _____ AND POLISHED, AND OFF SHE WENT. IT WAS AN
VERB (PAST TENSE)

EXHILARATING _____ AS THEY TACKLED THE _____ RUN OF
             NOUN   ADJECTIVE

MANY THEY EXPECTED TO _____ THIS DAY. THEY KNEW
                        VERB

TO STAY OUT OF THE _____ MARKED _____ AND OFF-
                  PLURAL NOUN   ADJECTIVE

LIMITS AND SO WOULD HAVE A _____ FILLED WITH _____ AND
                             NOUN   NOUN

_____. LATER, THEY LOOKED FORWARD TO _____ THEIR
NOUN   VERB—"ING"

TIME UP AT THE _____, _____ IN FRONT OF THE _____
              NOUN   VERB—"ING"   NOUN

AND WARMING THEMSELVES WITH _____ HOT _____.
                                 ADJECTIVE   NOUN

TRAVELIN' RHYMES

THIS IS A GREAT GAME TO PLAY AS YOU TRAVEL. YOU'LL NEED SOMEONE TO PLAY IT WITH, THOUGH, LIKE YOUR BROTHER OR SISTER OR FRIENDS.

BELOW IS A LIST OF WORD PAIRS THAT RHYME WITH EACH OTHER. YOUR JOB IS TO CALL OUT THE WORDS AND HAVE THE PLAYERS COME UP WITH THE SILLIEST RHYMES. WRITE THE BEST ON THE SPACES BELOW.

GLOVE, LOVE

BAKE, SNAKE

HORSE, COARSE

PLATE, GREAT

CAROL, BARREL

DINNER, THINNER

MEAT, FEET

SPELL, BELL

_____

_____

_____

_____

_____

_____

_____

it's a MYSTERY

THIS IS A GREAT GAME TO PLAY AS YOU TRAVEL. YOU'LL NEED SOMEONE TO PLAY IT WITH, THOUGH, LIKE YOUR BROTHER OR SISTER OR FRIENDS.

BELOW IS A LIST OF PHRASES THAT NEED TO BE COMPLETED. SHOW THIS PUZZLE TO EACH PLAYER, WHO PICKS A LETTER TO FILL IN THE BLANKS, AND THEN HAS TEN SECONDS TO GUESS THE PHRASE. MOVE ON TO EACH PLAYER UNTIL THE MYSTERY IS SOLVED! AS THE HOST OF THIS GAME, YOU GET TO CHECK OUT THE SOLUTION FROM THE ANSWER PAGES AT THE BACK (IF YOU NEED TO)!

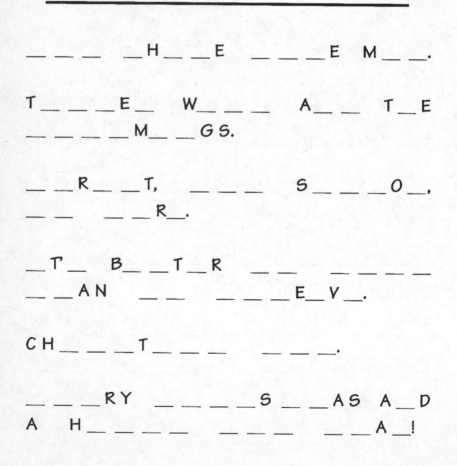

_ _ _ _H_ _E _ _ _E M_ _.

T_ _ _ _E_ W_ _ _ A_ _ T_E
_ _ _ _M_ _ G S.

_ _R_ _T, _ _ _ S_ _ _O_,
_ _ _ _R_.

_T_ B_ _T_R _ _ _ _ _ _
_ _AN _ _ _ _ _E_V_.

CH_ _ _ _T_ _ _ _ _ _.

_ _ _RY _ _ _ _ _S _ _AS A_D
A H_ _ _ _ _ _ _ _ _ _ A_!

80

THE PICTURES ARE YOUR CLUES. USE THE CIRCLED LETTERS TO COMPLETE THE PUZZLE BELOW.

WHAT'S REALLY, REALLY BIG AND COVERED WITH SNOW?

WHO, WHAT, WHERE

THIS IS A GREAT GAME TO PLAY AS YOU TRAVEL. YOU'LL NEED SOMEONE TO PLAY IT WITH, THOUGH, LIKE YOUR BROTHER OR SISTER OR FRIENDS.

BELOW IS A LIST OF QUESTIONS THAT NEED A "WHO, WHAT, OR WHERE" ANSWER. EACH PLAYER HAS TEN SECONDS TO ANSWER. AS THE HOST OF THIS GAME, YOU GET TO CHECK OUT THE SOLUTION FROM THE ANSWER PAGES AT THE BACK (IF YOU NEED TO)!

SKIS HELP GET YOU QUICKLY FROM THE TOP TO THE BOTTOM. *WHERE* ARE YOU? _____

THIS PERSON RECEIVED A MIRACLE, AND THE SAVIOR WAS BORN. *WHO* WAS IT? _____

THREE MEN FROM THE EAST VISITED THIS SMALL TOWN. *WHERE* WERE THEY? _____

IT IS MADE WAY UP NORTH, BUT YOU CAN MAKE ONE TOO. *WHAT* IS IT? _____

WITH THIS AND A HORSE YOU CAN GO ANYWHERE IN THE SNOW. *WHAT* IS IT? _____

ON THESE, YOU ENJOY THE SAME SPORT IN WINTER AND SUMMER. *WHAT* ARE THEY? _____

PICTURE MAKER

YOU MAKE THE PICTURE. DRAW THE IMAGE FROM EACH FRAME AT THE TOP IN THE FRAME BELOW WITH THE MATCHING NUMBER.

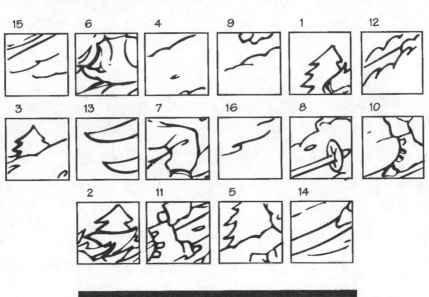

CAN YOU FIND THE WORDS?

ALL THESE
WORDS ARE HIDDEN IN
THE PUZZLE BELOW.
HAVE FUN!

ORNAMENT
TREE
MANGER
SNOWBALL
GIFTS

JESUS
TURKEY
CANDY
ICE
SCHOOL

```
        Y E
      S W C Q T U
    B H N I F P H S Y R
      Z O J L C V D F
      P T W T M N N Z L B
    F G U B K R A D T R E E
      M R A J C Z N G Z M
    Q Y K L T B E F G K H T
  K S G E L Y M G J U E V T D
      U Y D A T R K E L R
      L C K N M Y N G P S W K
  Z V Y R L S C H O O L U Q F
  R N O F W Z C J G I F T S Y
          G S
```

FIND THE FOUR

COMPLETE THE PUZZLE BELOW BY CROSSING OUT EVERY LETTER THAT APPEARS AT LEAST FOUR TIMES. USE THE REMAINING LETTERS TO COMPLETE THE SENTENCE.

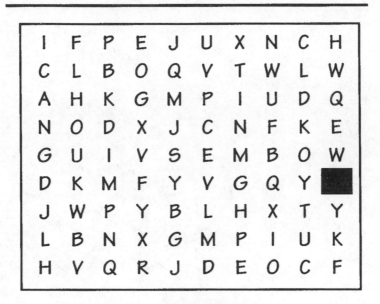

I	F	P	E	J	U	X	N	C	H
C	L	B	O	Q	V	T	W	L	W
A	H	K	G	M	P	I	U	D	Q
N	O	D	X	J	C	N	F	K	E
G	U	I	V	S	E	M	B	O	W
D	K	M	F	Y	V	G	Q	Y	■
J	W	P	Y	B	L	H	X	T	Y
L	B	N	X	G	M	P	I	U	K
H	V	Q	R	J	D	E	O	C	F

CHRISTMAS IS A TIME TO _ _ _ _ _

THINKING ABOUT OTHERS!

LESS SHALL BE FIRST

PLACE THE WORDS BELOW INTO THE PUZZLE ACCORDING TO THE NUMBER OF LETTERS IN EACH WORD, BEGINNING WITH THE WORD THAT HAS THE FEWEST LETTERS. THEN UNSCRAMBLE THE CIRCLED LETTERS TO COMPLETE THE ANSWER BELOW.

DINNER
GIVE
HOLIDAYS
SKI

PRESENT
BETHLEHEM
IGLOO

TO YOU, A ___ ___ ___ ___ ___ ___ IS BORN.

REALLY SILLY STORIES

YOU CAN PLAY THIS GAME BY YOURSELF, BUT IT'S A LOT MORE FUN TO PLAY WITH OTHERS.

ASK EACH PLAYER TO CALL OUT THE KIND OF WORD INDICATED IN EACH SPACE—A NOUN OR ADJECTIVE OR ADVERB, FOR EXAMPLE—AND PLACE THAT WORD IN THE APPROPRIATE SPACE. DO NOT TELL ANYONE WHAT THE STORY IS ABOUT— IT'S MORE FUN THAT WAY!

BELOW YOU'LL FIND A DESCRIPTION OF WHAT VERBS, NOUNS, ADJECTIVES, ADVERBS, ETC., ARE—JUST IN CASE YOU NEED A LITTLE HELP.

<u>VERB</u>: AN ACTION WORD, LIKE *WALK, RUN,* OR *FLY*. MAY BE *WALKED, RAN,* OR *FLEW,* IF <u>PAST TENSE</u> IS CALLED FOR.

<u>ADVERB</u>: MODIFIES A VERB AND USUALLY ENDS IN "LY." *SLOWLY* AND *CAREFULLY* ARE A COUPLE OF EXAMPLES.

<u>NOUN</u>: A PERSON, PLACE, OR THING, LIKE *BOY, BOAT,* OR *CAR*.

<u>ADJECTIVE</u>: DESCRIBES SOMEONE OR SOME-THING. *DIRTY, SILLY,* AND *BIG* ARE A FEW EXAMPLES.

<u>PLACE</u>: COULD BE A *COUNTRY* OR *CITY,* ETC.

<u>PLURAL</u>: MORE THAN ONE ITEM, SUCH AS *GIRLS* IS THE PLURAL OF *GIRL*.

NOW MOVE ON TO THE FOLLOWING PAGE TO PLAY THIS REALLY SILLY GAME!

REALLY SILLY STORIES

DON'T LOOK AT THE STORY BELOW. INSTEAD, FILL IN THE
BLANKS IN THE LIST BELOW WITH THE REQUIRED WORDS.
THEN FILL IN THE BLANKS IN THE STORY AND GET READY TO
LAUGH UNCONTROLLABLY!

NOUN _____   NOUN _____
ADJECTIVE _____   NOUN _____
PLURAL NOUN _____   NOUN _____
VERB—PAST TENSE _____   PLURAL NOUN _____
VERB ENDING IN "ING"   NOUN _____
_____   NOUN _____
ADJECTIVE _____   PLURAL NOUN _____
VERB ENDING IN "ING"   NOUN _____
_____   VERB _____
NOUN _____   ADJECTIVE _____
PLURAL NOUN _____   PLURAL NOUN _____
NOUN _____   ADJECTIVE _____

THE _____ WAS GETTING _____ AND HIGHER. KEVIN AND
   NOUN   ADJECTIVE

HIS THREE _____ HAD _____ THE MORNING _____ AN
     PLURAL NOUN VERB (PAST TENSE)   VERB—"ING"

_____ SNOW FORT AND WERE NOW _____ UP ON
ADJECTIVE   VERB—"ING"

THE "AMMUNITION" THEY WOULD NEED. WITH THE _____
                                       NOUN

OF _____ THEY WERE AMASSING, THE OTHER _____
   PLURAL NOUN   NOUN

WOULD HAVE NO _____ AGAINST THEM IN THIS _____
             NOUN   NOUN

_____ THAT WAS SURE TO MAKE HISTORY! BOTH _____
NOUN   PLURAL NOUN

HAD AGREED ON A _____ IT WOULD BEGIN, AND THAT LEFT
              NOUN

THEM AN _____ TO GO. AS THEY CONTINUED TO MAKE
        NOUN

_____ THEY DISCUSSED THEIR _____. THE OTHER GUYS
PLURAL NOUN   NOUN

WOULDN'T _____ A CHANCE! THEN, SUDDENLY A _____
      VERB   ADJECTIVE

OF _____ CAME AT THEM. IT WAS A _____ ATTACK!
  PLURAL NOUN   ADJECTIVE

PICTURE CLUES

THE PICTURES ARE YOUR ONLY CLUES TO COMPLETING THIS CROSSWORD. THIS IS A BIT OF A BRAIN TEASER.

LET'S MAZE AROUND

THE CHURCH PLAY HAS ALMOST BEGUN. HELP THE GANG
FIND THEIR WAY IN THE DARK.

DON'T LEAVE IT SCRAMBLED!

UNSCRAMBLE EACH WORD. THEN USE THE CIRCLED LETTERS TO COMPLETE THE PUZZLE BELOW... AND I HOPE IT DOESN'T HURT YOUR EYES!

YVNREOEE   ELVOS   ICVEGERIN

_ _ _ _ _ _ _ _   _ _ _ _ _   _ _ (_) _ _ _ _ _ _

FTIGS   TA   MRAHCTSSI   NDA   MEOS

_ _ _ _ _   _ _   _ _ (_) _ _ _ _ _ _   _ _ _   _ (_) _ _

VEHA   NVEE   ROSEEDVCDI   HET   OYJ

_ _ (_) _   _ _ _ _   _ _ _ _ _ _ _ _ _   _ _ _   _ _ _

AHTT   MESCO   NI   NIIGVG   SGFTI.

_ _ _ _   _ _ (_) _ _   _ _   _ _ _ _ _ _   _ _ _ _ _ .

IHTS   TUSMOC   SI   EASDB   NO

_ _ _ _   _ _ _ _ _ _   _ _   _ _ (_) _ _   _ _

GTFIS   GOBRUTH   OT   HTE   OWBENRN

_ _ _ _ _   _ _ _ _ _ _ _   _ _   _ _ _   _ _ (_) _ _ _ _

EUSJS.

_ _ _ _ _ .

( )( )( )( )   ( )( )( )   OR MAGI,

KINGS FROM THE EAST, CARRIED GIFTS FOR THE LORD.

91

TRAVELIN' RHYMES

THIS IS A GREAT GAME TO PLAY AS YOU TRAVEL. YOU'LL NEED SOMEONE TO PLAY IT WITH, THOUGH, LIKE YOUR BROTHER OR SISTER OR FRIENDS.

BELOW IS A LIST OF WORD PAIRS THAT RHYME WITH EACH OTHER. YOUR JOB IS TO CALL OUT THE WORDS AND HAVE THE PLAYERS COME UP WITH THE SILLIEST RHYMES. WRITE THE BEST ON THE SPACES BELOW.

MERRY, DAIRY   RABBIT, HABIT
TOYS, BOYS   SLIDE, HIDE
CAT, MAT   PINE, DINE
DEER, STEER   SING, RING

_____

_____

_____

_____

_____

_____

_____

LET'S MAZE AROUND

THE KIDS HAVE BEEN OUT PLAYING ALL DAY, AND THEY ARE
FAMISHED! THEY'VE JUST BEEN CALLED FOR DINNER—HELP
THEM FIND THE SHORTEST WAY HOME.

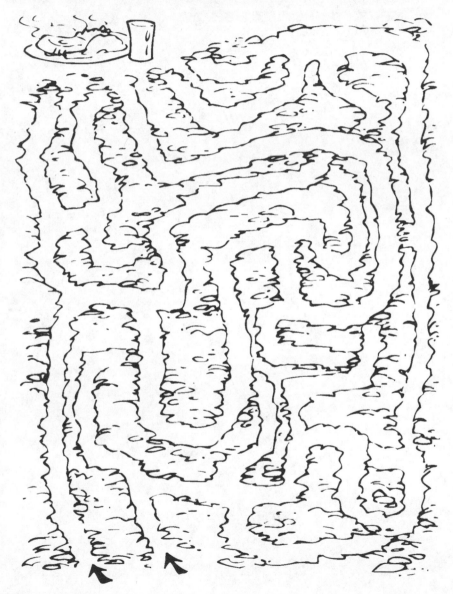

ALL JUMBLED UP

HEY . . . THIS ONE WILL BE FUN!
FIND THE OPPOSITE OF EACH WORD,
THEN USE THE CIRCLED LETTERS TO
COMPLETE THE PUZZLE BELOW.

SICK _ _ _ ⊘ _

RUN ⊘ _ _ _

BUY ⊘ _ _ _

UNWRAP _ ⊘ _ _

TEACH _ _ _ ⊘

FAST _ _ ⊘ _

SHRINK _ _ ⊘ _ _

LAST ⊘ _ _ _

A PLACE OF REFUGE:

◯ ◯ ◯ ◯   ◯ ◯ ◯ ◯

REALLY SILLY STORIES

YOU CAN PLAY THIS GAME BY YOURSELF, BUT IT'S A LOT MORE FUN TO PLAY WITH OTHERS.

ASK EACH PLAYER TO CALL OUT THE KIND OF WORD INDICATED IN EACH SPACE—A NOUN OR ADJECTIVE OR ADVERB, FOR EXAMPLE—AND PLACE THAT WORD IN THE APPROPRIATE SPACE. DO NOT TELL ANYONE WHAT THE STORY IS ABOUT— IT'S MORE FUN THAT WAY!

BELOW YOU'LL FIND A DESCRIPTION OF WHAT VERBS, NOUNS, ADJECTIVES, ADVERBS, ETC., ARE—JUST IN CASE YOU NEED A LITTLE HELP.

<u>VERB</u>: AN ACTION WORD, LIKE *WALK, RUN,* OR *FLY.* MAY BE *WALKED, RAN,* OR *FLEW,* IF <u>PAST TENSE</u> IS CALLED FOR.

<u>ADVERB</u>: MODIFIES A VERB AND USUALLY ENDS IN "LY." *SLOWLY* AND *CAREFULLY* ARE A COUPLE OF EXAMPLES.

<u>NOUN</u>: A PERSON, PLACE, OR THING, LIKE *BOY, BOAT,* OR *CAR.*

<u>ADJECTIVE</u>: DESCRIBES SOMEONE OR SOMETHING. *DIRTY, SILLY,* AND *BIG* ARE A FEW EXAMPLES.

<u>PLACE</u>: COULD BE A *COUNTRY* OR *CITY,* ETC.

<u>PLURAL</u>: MORE THAN ONE ITEM, SUCH AS *GIRLS* IS THE PLURAL OF *GIRL.*

NOW MOVE ON TO THE FOLLOWING PAGE TO PLAY THIS REALLY SILLY GAME!

REALLY SILLY STORIES

DON'T LOOK AT THE STORY BELOW. INSTEAD, FILL IN THE BLANKS IN THE LIST BELOW WITH THE REQUIRED WORDS. THEN FILL IN THE BLANKS IN THE STORY AND GET READY TO LAUGH UNCONTROLLABLY!

NAME _____   PLURAL NOUN _____

ADJECTIVE _____   ADJECTIVE _____

NOUN _____   NOUN _____

VERB (PAST TENSE) _____   ADJECTIVE _____

_____   NOUN _____

VERB _____   VERB (PAST TENSE) _____

NOUN _____   _____

NOUN _____   NOUN _____

NOUN _____   NOUN _____

NOUN _____   VERB _____

ADJECTIVE _____   ADJECTIVE _____

     NOUN _____

JEFFEREY AND _____, ALONG WITH HER _____
            NAME   ADJECTIVE

_____, JIMMY HAD JUST _____ AT MAPLE TREE PARK
NOUN   VERB (PAST TENSE)

AND WERE BEGINNING THE LONG _____ UP THE WESTWARD
                                VERB

_____. PULLING THE FRESHLY POLISHED _____ BEHIND
NOUN   NOUN

THEM, THEY HAD IN MIND TO SPEND THE _____ MAKING
                                NOUN

_____ DOWN THIS _____ HILL. THERE WERE FEW
NOUN   ADJECTIVE

_____, AS IT WAS STILL _____ IN THE MORNING. AT
PLURAL NOUN   ADJECTIVE

LAST THEY ARRIVED AT THE _____ AND DECIDED TO MOVE
                          NOUN

OVER _____ _____ OR SO, AS ALONG THE WAY, THEY
      ADJECTIVE   NOUN

HAD _____ A RATHER NASTY LOOKING _____ UNDER
VERB (PAST TENSE)   NOUN

THE _____ WHICH THEY WANTED TO _____.
     NOUN   VERB

FINALLY, THEY WERE OFF! WHAT A _____ _____
                           ADJECTIVE   NOUN

THIS WAS GOING TO BE.

FIND THE FOUR

COMPLETE THE PUZZLE BELOW BY CROSSING OUT EVERY LETTER THAT APPEARS AT LEAST FOUR TIMES. USE THE REMAINING LETTERS TO COMPLETE THE SENTENCE.

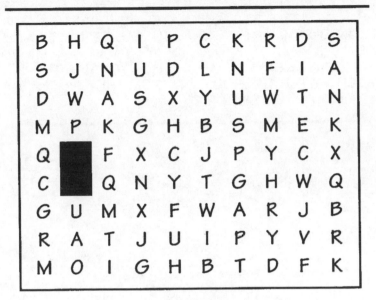

```
B H Q I P C K R D S
S J N U D L N F I A
D W A S X Y U W T N
M P K G H B S M E K
Q   F X C J P Y C X
C   Q N Y T G H W Q
G U M X F W A R J B
R A T J U I P Y V R
M O I G H B T D F K
```

JESUS WAS BORN BECAUSE OF GOD'S LOVE FOR YOU! IN HIM, YOU TOO CAN _ _ _ _ OTHERS.

it's a MYSTERY

THIS IS A GREAT GAME TO PLAY AS YOU TRAVEL. YOU'LL NEED SOMEONE TO PLAY IT WITH, THOUGH, LIKE YOUR BROTHER OR SISTER OR FRIENDS.

BELOW IS A LIST OF PHRASES THAT NEED TO BE COMPLETED. SHOW THIS PUZZLE TO EACH PLAYER, WHO PICKS A LETTER TO FILL IN THE BLANKS, AND THEN HAS TEN SECONDS TO GUESS THE PHRASE. MOVE ON TO EACH PLAYER UNTIL THE MYSTERY IS SOLVED! AS THE HOST OF THIS GAME, YOU GET TO CHECK OUT THE SOLUTION FROM THE ANSWER PAGES AT THE BACK (IF YOU NEED TO)!

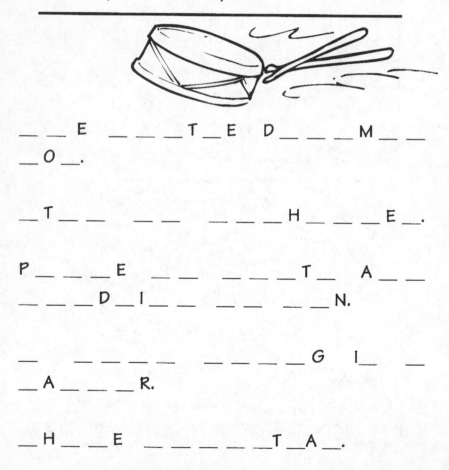

_ _ E _ _ _ T _ E D _ _ _ M _ _ _ O _.

_ T _ _ _ _ _ _ _ _ H _ _ _ E _.

P _ _ _ E _ _ _ _ _ T _ A _ _ _ _ _ D _ I _ _ _ _ _ _ _ N.

_ _ _ _ _ _ _ _ _ _ G I _ _ _ A _ _ _ R.

_ H _ _ E _ _ _ _ _ _ T _ A _.

LETTER CLUES

TO DECODE THIS MESSAGE FROM GOD, YOU'LL NEED TO TAKE THE LETTER FROM EACH NUMBERED CLUE AND MATCH IT TO THE NUMBERED SPACE IN THE PUZZLE BELOW.

1. IT CAN BE FOUND IN *LAST* BUT NOT IN *LOST*.

    _____

2. LOOK FOR IT ONCE IN BOTH *TOY* AND IN *YELL*.

    _____

3. THIRD IN PLACE IN BOTH *RENT* AND IN *LENT*.

    _____

4. IT CAN BE FOUND IN *SONG* BUT NOT IN *SANG*.

    _____

5. IT DOUBLES BOTH *BOOTS* AND *TOBOGGANS*.

    _____

6. THIS LETTER BEGINS *ROUND* AND ENDS *HOUR*.

    _____

7. IT IS FOUND AT THE BEGINNING OF *JAM* AND *JOY*.

    _____

"W H E __   T H E __   __ __ W   T H E   __ T __ __,
     3   2   5 1   5 1 6

T H E __   W E __ E   __ V E __ __ __ __ E D.   __ __
    2   6   4   6 7 4 2   4 3

C __ M I __ G __ T __   T H E   H __ U __ E,   T H E __
  4   3   4   4   5   2

__ __ W   T H E   C H I L D   W I T H   H I __   M __ T H E __
5 1   5   4   6

M __ __ __,   __ __ D   T H E __   B __ W E D   D __ W __
  1 6 2   1 3   2   4   4   3

__ __ D   W __ __ __ HIPED   HIM."
1 3   4 6 5

MATTHEW 2:10–11

CAN YOU FIND THE WORDS?

ALL THESE WORDS ARE HIDDEN IN THE PUZZLE BELOW. HAVE FUN!

SILENT
HOLY
CANDLE
CONCERT
HOLIDAY

TOYS
MOUNTAIN
BELLS
TINSEL
HOLLY

```
                          W T Y
        R J K M Y K S Q H F H
      T R Z M T L T G W K O Z O
    B E L L S O D L I Z B L S L
    H W E Q H K U Y U N G L A I
    Q M S L U P F N H L S Y H D
    K G I B F K G L T T L E W A
    D Z L S Q T V J R A Q T L Y
    K T E D K H A E T W I R B J
    C A N D L E C P E V K N U W
    E B T Q F N K Z R F Q D G L
    L W U Y O G W M S L B N Q T
    M P F C E J L W F T P G Y P
    S G                T O Y S
```

CAN YOU PICTURE IT.

THE PICTURES ARE YOUR CLUES. USE THE CIRCLED LETTERS TO COMPLETE THE PUZZLE BELOW.

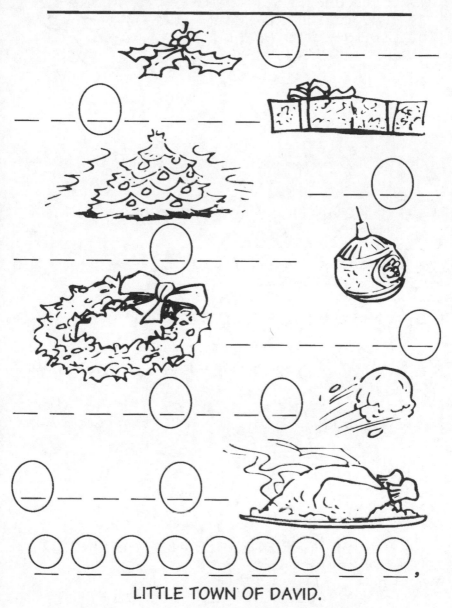

LITTLE TOWN OF DAVID.

DON'T LEAVE IT SCRAMBLED!

UNSCRAMBLE EACH WORD. THEN USE THE CIRCLED LETTERS TO COMPLETE THE PUZZLE BELOW... AND I HOPE IT DOESN'T HURT YOUR EYES!

M I R H S T C A S   S I   O S   C M H U   F N U

_ _ _ _ _ _ _ _   _ _   _ _   _ _ _ _   _ _ _

N A D   E Y R V E   E R Y A   V A E E S L   I G S T N A L

_ _ _   _ _ _ _ _   _(_)_ _   _ _ _ _ _ _   _ _ _ _ _ _ _

E R S I M M O E.   P G E I N K E   N I   D I M N   O T

_ _ _ _ _ _ _ _.   _ _ _ _ _ _   _ _   _ _ _   _ _

E B   N C O T R E A I E D S   O T   O T E S H

_ _   _ _ _ _(_)_ _ _ _   _ _(_)   _ _(_) _

N R A O D U   O Y U   S A L V E E   U Y O   H W T I

(_)_ _ _ _   _ _ _   _ _ _ _ _ _   _ _ _   _ _ _ _

M M O E E S I R   F O   A   R V Y E   I C P E A S L

_ _ _ _ _ _ (_)_   _ _   _   _ _ _ _   _ _ _ _ _ _

I D K N.

_ _ _ _.

A BLESSED CHRISTMAS IS IN BEING KIND TO

◯ ◯ ◯ ◯ ◯ ◯ .

PICTURE MAKER

YOU MAKE THE PICTURE. DRAW THE IMAGE FROM EACH
FRAME AT THE TOP IN THE FRAME BELOW WITH THE
MATCHING NUMBER.

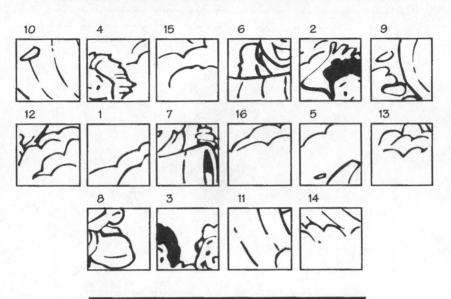

FIND THE FOUR

COMPLETE THE PUZZLE BELOW BY CROSSING OUT EVERY LETTER THAT APPEARS AT LEAST FOUR TIMES. USE THE REMAINING LETTERS TO COMPLETE THE SENTENCE.

```
N  H  I  S  T     P  K  V  R  D
A  L  Q  B  Z  W  X  U  S  N
P  W  Y  M           J  B  Z  L
D  O  J           A  W  Q
N  X  K           P  A  B
J  D  Z           F  S  V
C  X  L  Y        D  I  Y  E
V  B  S  P  G  Y  Z  I  N  K
K  Q  I  L  W  J  Q  V  A  X
```

THE WINTER SEASON IS FULL OF __ __ __ __ FUN
AND EXCITEMENT, BUT DON'T __ __ __ __ __ __
WHAT IT'S REALLY ABOUT.

104

REALLY SILLY STORIES

YOU CAN PLAY THIS GAME BY YOURSELF, BUT IT'S A LOT MORE FUN TO PLAY WITH OTHERS.

ASK EACH PLAYER TO CALL OUT THE KIND OF WORD INDICATED IN EACH SPACE—A NOUN OR ADJECTIVE OR ADVERB, FOR EXAMPLE—AND PLACE THAT WORD IN THE APPROPRIATE SPACE. DO NOT TELL ANYONE WHAT THE STORY IS ABOUT—IT'S MORE FUN THAT WAY!

BELOW YOU'LL FIND A DESCRIPTION OF WHAT VERBS, NOUNS, ADJECTIVES, ADVERBS, ETC., ARE—JUST IN CASE YOU NEED A LITTLE HELP.

VERB: AN ACTION WORD, LIKE *WALK*, *RUN*, OR *FLY*. MAY BE *WALKED*, *RAN*, OR *FLEW*, IF <u>PAST TENSE</u> IS CALLED FOR.

ADVERB: MODIFIES A VERB AND USUALLY ENDS IN "LY." *SLOWLY* AND *CAREFULLY* ARE A COUPLE OF EXAMPLES.

NOUN: A PERSON, PLACE, OR THING, LIKE *BOY*, *BOAT*, OR *CAR*.

ADJECTIVE: DESCRIBES SOMEONE OR SOME-THING. *DIRTY*, *SILLY*, AND *BIG* ARE A FEW EXAMPLES.

PLACE: COULD BE A *COUNTRY* OR *CITY*, ETC.

PLURAL: MORE THAN ONE ITEM, SUCH AS *GIRLS* IS THE PLURAL OF *GIRL*.

NOW MOVE ON TO THE FOLLOWING PAGE TO PLAY THIS REALLY SILLY GAME!

REALLY SILLY STORIES

DON'T LOOK AT THE STORY BELOW. INSTEAD, FILL IN THE BLANKS IN THE LIST BELOW WITH THE REQUIRED WORDS. THEN FILL IN THE BLANKS IN THE STORY AND GET READY TO LAUGH UNCONTROLLABLY!

NOUN _____   VERB (PAST TENSE)
ADJECTIVE _____   _____
NOUN _____   ADVERB_____
NOUN _____   NOUN _____
VERB ENDING IN "ING"   NOUN _____
_____   NOUN _____
NOUN _____   PLURAL NOUN _____
NOUN _____   PLURAL NOUN _____
ADJECTIVE _____   ADJECTIVE _____
NOUN _____   VERB _____
                             PLURAL NOUN _____

A _____ OF _____ SNOW COVERED THE _____
  NOUN   ADJECTIVE   NOUN

ON THIS CHRISTMAS _____. CHILDREN WERE _____
                       NOUN   VERB—"ING"

IN EVERY _____ AND EACH WAS FILLED WITH AWE AND
           NOUN

_____ AS THEY LOOKED _____. WHAT A BEAUTIFUL
 NOUN   ADJECTIVE

_____ THAT WOULD ACCOMPANY THEM AS THEY
   NOUN

_____ TO OPEN PRESENTS _____ THIS
VERB (PAST TENSE)   ADVERB

_____. WHAT A WONDERFUL _____ TO BE SO
  NOUN   NOUN

BLESSED WITH _____ AND PLENTY AND SECURITY. THEIR
           NOUN

_____ WOULD REMIND THEM THAT THERE WERE
  PLURAL NOUN

SO MANY _____ NOT SO _____ AND THAT
        PLURAL NOUN   ADJECTIVE

THEY SHOULD BE SURE TO _____ THEM IN MIND AND IN
                      VERB

THEIR _____.
    PLURAL NOUN

JUST A REGULAR OLD CROSSWORD!

ACROSS

1. THINKING OF OTHERS
2. CHRISTMAS SCENE
3. TYPE OF TREE
4. CONSUMING FOOD
5. NICE TO WALK IN

DOWN

1. KIND TO OTHERS
2. TREE ORNAMENT
3. CHRISTMAS MEAT
4. TO STUMBLE
5. WIFE OF A CARPENTER

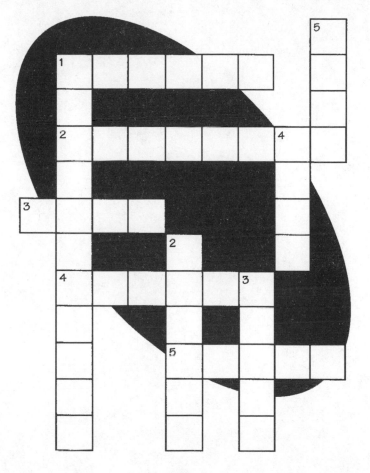

HERE ARE THE
ANSWERS!

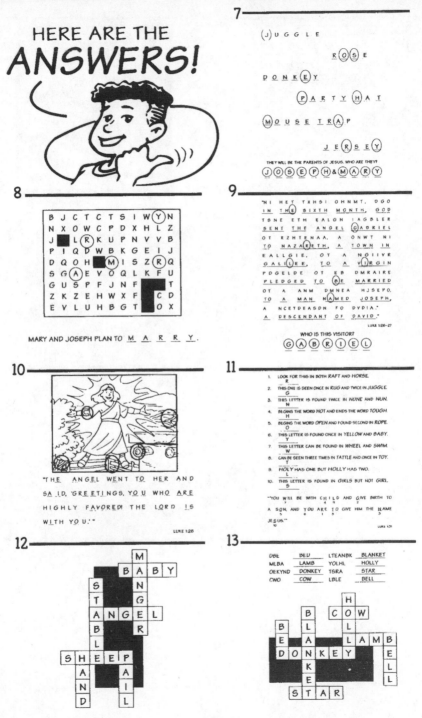

7

(J) U G G L E

R (O) S E

D O N K (E) Y

(P) A R T Y (H) A T

(M) O U S E T R (A) P

J E (R) S E (Y)

THEY WILL BE THE PARENTS OF JESUS. WHO ARE THEY?

(J) (O) (S) (E) (P) (H) & (M) (A) (R) (Y)

8

B	J	C	T	C	T	S	I	W	(Y)	N
N	X	O	W	C	P	D	X	H	L	Z
J	■	L	(R)	K	U	P	N	V	V	B
P	I	Q	D	W	B	K	G	E	I	J
D	Q	O	H	(M)	I	S	Z	(R)	Q
S	G	(A)	E	V	O	Q	L	K	F	U
G	U	■	P	F	J	N	F	■	T
Z	K	Z	E	H	W	X	F	C	D
E	V	L	U	H	B	G	T	■	O	X

MARY AND JOSEPH PLAN TO __M__ __A__ __R__ __R__ __Y__.

9

"NI HET TXHSI OHNMT, DGO
IN T H E SIXTH MONTH, GOD
TSNE ETH EALGN IAGBLER
SENT THE ANGEL (G)ABRIEL
OT RZHTENAA, A ONWT NI
TO NAZA(R)ETH, A TOWN IN
EALLGIE, OT A NGIIVR
GALI(L)EE, TO A V(I)RGIN
PDGELDE OT EB DMRAIRE
PLEDGED TO (B)E MARRIED
OT A ANM DMNEA HJSEPO.
TO A MAN N(A)MED JOSEPH,
A NCETDEASDN FO DVDIA."
A DESCENDANT OF DAVID."
LUKE 1:26–27

WHO IS THIS VISITOR?

(G) (A) (B) (R) (I) (E) (L)

10

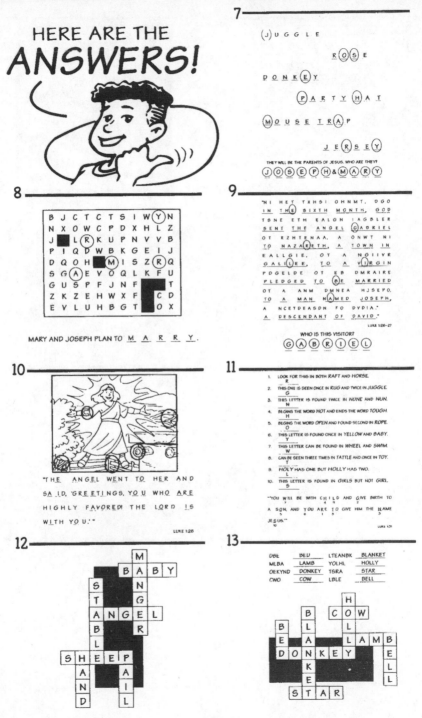

"THE ANGEL WENT TO HER AND
SAID, 'GREETINGS, YOU WHO ARE
HIGHLY FAVORED! THE LORD IS
WITH YOU.'"
LUKE 1:28

11

1. LOOK FOR THIS IN BOTH RAFT AND HORSE.
   R
2. THIS ONE IS SEEN ONCE IN RUG AND TWICE IN JUGGLE.
   G
3. THIS LETTER IS FOUND TWICE IN NUNE AND NUN.
   N
4. BEGINS THE WORD HOT AND ENDS THE WORD TOUGH.
   H
5. BEGINS THE WORD OPEN AND FOUND SECOND IN ROPE.
   O
6. THIS LETTER IS FOUND ONCE IN YELLOW AND BABY.
   Y
7. THIS LETTER CAN BE FOUND IN WHEEL AND SWIM.
   W
8. CAN BE SEEN THREE TIMES IN TATTLE AND ONCE IN TOY.
   T
9. HOLY HAS ONE BUT HOLLY HAS TWO.
   L
10. THIS LETTER IS FOUND IN GIRLS BUT NOT GIRL.
    S

"YOU WILL BE WITH C H I L D AND G I V E BIRTH TO
A S O N, AND Y O U ARE T O GIVE HIM THE N A M E
JE S U S.'"
LUKE 1:31

12

			M	
	B	A	B	Y
S		N		
T		G		
A	N	G	E	L
B		R		
L				
S H E E	P		
A		A		
N		I		
D		L		

13

DBE	BED	LTEANBK	BLANKET
MLBA	LAMB	YOLHL	HOLLY
OEKYND	DONKEY	TSRA	STAR
CWO	COW	LBLE	BELL

H
B C O W
B L O
E A L L A M B
D O N K E Y E
N L
E L
STAR

109

14

```
H K F T O R P J Y V M
N V Q Z C W G V M E S
P B A S V Q U T Z E K
U X M              L R
G E O          O P W
S N T J F G X Z B Y F
D R Q I K R S A W J U
J Y U P N M O G N Q B
A T F W E B X A K Y X
```

MARY FINDS OUT THAT HER COUSIN, ELIZABETH,
WILL ALSO HAVE A C H I L D .

16

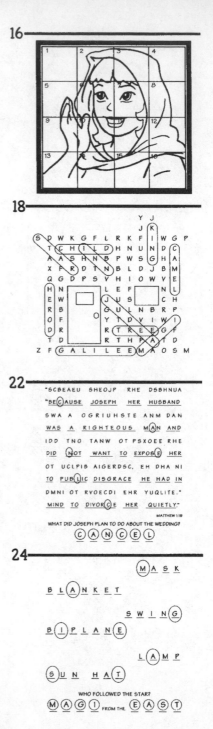

17

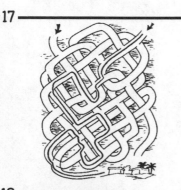

18

```
                    Y J
                    J K
S D W K G F L R K F I W G P
T C H I L D H N U G D H C
A A S H N B P W S N G H A
X F R D T N B L D J B M M
Q G D P S V H I O W V E E
          L E F     N C L
H N W     J U S     H P
E O W B F G U I N B R P
R D F R   Y T D V I W I
O E F R   R T R E E G T D
D T       R T H P A I D
Z F G A L I L E E M A O S M
```

19

"WHEN E L I Z A B E T H H E A R D
M A R Y'S G R E E T I N G, T H E B A B Y
L E A P E D I N H E R W O M B, A N D
E L I Z A B E T H W A S F I L L E D
W I T H T H E H O L Y S P I R I T."

LUKE 1:41

22

"SCBEAEU SHEOJP RHE DSBHNUA
"BECAUSE JOSEPH HER HUSBAND
SWA A OGRIUHSTE ANM DAN
WAS A RIGHTEOUS MAN AND
IDD TNO TANW OT PSXOEE RHE
DID NOT WANT TO EXPOSE HER
OT UCLPIB AIGERDSC, EH DHA NI
TO PUBLIC DISGRACE HE HAD IN
DMNI OT RVOECDI EHR YUQLITE."
MIND TO DIVORCE HER QUIETLY."

MATTHEW 1:19

WHAT DID JOSEPH PLAN TO DO ABOUT THE WEDDING?
C A N C E L

23

THE LORD JESUS WAS BORN
IN BETHLEHEM.

THE MAGI BROUGHT GIFTS.

THERE WAS NO ROOM AT
THE INN.

A GREAT HOST OF ANGELS
APPEARED.

MARY, THE MOTHER OF THE
BABY JESUS.

A CHILD IS BORN, WHO
IS CHRIST, THE LORD.

24

M A S K

B L A N K E T

S W I N G

B I P L A N E

L A M P

S U N H A T

WHO FOLLOWED THE STAR?
M A G I FROM THE E A S T

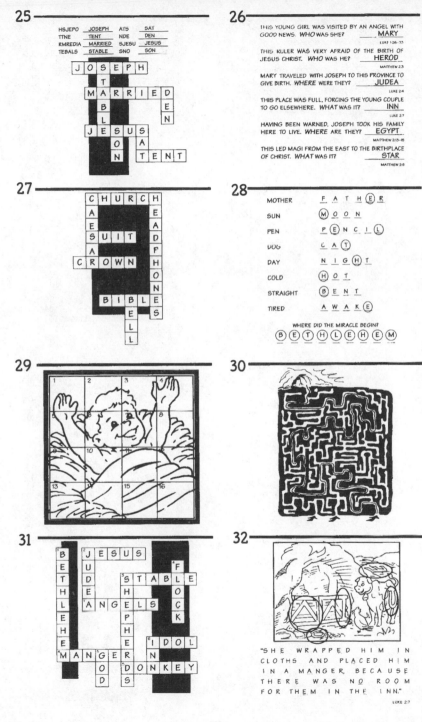

25

HSJEPO	JOSEPH	ATS	SAT
TTNE	TENT	NDE	DEN
RMREDIA	MARRIED	SJESU	JESUS
TEBALS	STABLE	SNO	SON

Crossword:
JOSEPH
MARRIED
JESUS
TENT

26

THIS YOUNG GIRL WAS VISITED BY AN ANGEL WITH GOOD NEWS. *WHO* WAS SHE? __MARY__
LUKE 1:26-33

THIS RULER WAS VERY AFRAID OF THE BIRTH OF JESUS CHRIST. *WHO* WAS HE? __HEROD__
MATTHEW 2:3

MARY TRAVELED WITH JOSEPH TO THIS PROVINCE TO GIVE BIRTH. *WHERE* WERE THEY? __JUDEA__
LUKE 2:4

THIS PLACE WAS FULL, FORCING THE YOUNG COUPLE TO GO ELSEWHERE. *WHAT* WAS IT? __INN__
LUKE 2:7

HAVING BEEN WARNED, JOSEPH TOOK HIS FAMILY HERE TO LIVE. *WHERE* ARE THEY? __EGYPT__
MATTHEW 2:13-15

THIS LED MAGI FROM THE EAST TO THE BIRTHPLACE OF CHRIST. *WHAT* WAS IT? __STAR__
MATTHEW 2:9

27

Crossword:
CHURCH
SUIT
CROWN
BIBLE
(HEADPHONES, BELL)

28

MOTHER	F A T H (E) R
SUN	(M) O O N
PEN	P (E) N C I (L)
DOG	C A (T)
DAY	N I G (H) T
COLD	(H) O T
STRAIGHT	(B) E N T
TIRED	A W A K (E)

WHERE DID THE MIRACLE BEGIN?
(B)(E)(T)(H)(L)(E)(H)(E)(M)

29

30

31

Crossword:
BETHLEHEM
JESUS
JUDEA
STABLE
ANGELS
SHEPHERDS
FLOCK
MANGER
IDOL
DONKEY
WOOD

32

"SHE WRAPPED HIM IN CLOTHS AND PLACED HIM IN A MANGER, BECAUSE THERE WAS NO ROOM FOR THEM IN THE INN."
LUKE 2:7

1. THIS LETTER BEGINS *HAIR* AND ENDS *ROUGH.*
   H
2. FOUND SECOND TO LAST IN BOTH *LOVE* AND *LEAVE.*
   V
3. FOUND ONCE IN *CRUMB* AND TWICE IN *ACCEPT.*
   C
4. THIS ONE'S TWICE IN *EFFECT* BUT ONCE IN *FAIR.*
   F
5. YOU'LL FIND THIS ONE IN *BEST* BUT NOT IN *BUST.*
   E
6. YOU'LL FIND THIS TWICE IN *BABY* AND ONCE IN *BOAT.*
   B
7. THIS LETTER BEGINS *GOAT* AND ENDS *JOG.*
   G

"AND T H E R E   W E R E   S H E P H E R D S
LI V I N G OUT IN T H E   F I E L DS N E A R B Y,
KEEPING WAT C H   OVER   THEIR
F L O CKS AT N I G H T."

LUKE 2:8

```
M V X K M Q W R I Y
H G B Z S C C K E X
R P J B F Z Q V H R
C T Q W H ■ Z C D K
U K D J U I J S V T
W O M Z O X M D O Y
S N U P Y L P Y B F
F P X O D R T F Q V
I W T I A J S U H B
```

AN A N G E L APPEARS TO THE SHEPHERDS.

ISHHGTE	HIGHEST	WCAHT	WATCH
ONTW	TOWN	SHTO	HOST
GYLRO	GLORY	DLGA	GLAD
VLNYEEAH	HEAVENLY	ISH	HIS
DLRO	LORD	AEHRT	EARTH
HNEOS	SHONE	ERATH	HEART

(crossword grid containing: GLAD, TOWN, HO, EARTH, HOST, H, A, C, I, V, E, SHONE, N, HIS, EART, L, GLORY, S, T)

37

SHEPHERDS WERE AT WORK, LOOKING AFTER THEIR SHEEP. *WHERE* WERE THEY? ___ FIELDS
LUKE 2:8

SUDDENLY, SOMETHING SHONE ALL AROUND THEM. *WHAT* WAS IT? ___ GLORY OF THE LORD
LUKE 2:9

HE BROUGHT THEM *GOOD NEWS* OF GREAT JOY FOR ALL PEOPLE. *WHO* WAS HE? ___ ANGEL
LUKE 2:10

A SAVIOR HAD BEEN BORN WHO WAS CHRIST, THE LORD. *WHERE* WAS HE BORN? TOWN OF DAVID
LUKE 2:11

ALL GLORY WAS GIVEN TO HIM BY THE ANGELS AND ALL MEN. *WHO* WAS HE? ___ GOD
LUKE 2:14

HE HAD NO BED, BUT THEY FOUND A PLACE TO LAY HIM DOWN. *WHAT* WAS IT? ___ MANGER
LUKE 2:12

PEACE WAS GIVEN TO THEM ON WHOM RESTED THE FAVOR OF GOD. *WHO* WERE THEY? ___ MEN
LUKE 2:14

(picture grid numbered 1–16 with shepherd scene)

39

"LDSUYNDE A RTEAG MCAYNOP FO
SUDDENLY A G R E A T COMPANY OF

HET VHNEEAYL STHO EEAARPDP WHTI
THE H E AVENLY HOST APPEARED WITH

ETH NEALG, IISPRGAN DGO NDA
THE A NGEL, PRAISING GOD AND

NASYGI, 'OGLRY OT ODG NI HET
SAYING, 'GLORY TO GOD IN THE

EIHSTGH, NAD NO TERAH ECPEA
HIGHE S T, AND ON EARTH P EACE

OT NME NO OWMH ISH AFRVO
TO MEN ON WHOM H I S FAVOR

TRSES.'"
RESTS.'"

LUKE 2:13-14

THE HOST OF ANGELS
P R A I S E D GOD.

(crossword grid: BETHLEHEM, T, P, A, B, H, R, A, B, I, R, C, Y, G, I, E, H, F, SHINE, J, I, HOST, E, DAVID, S, E, PRAISING, H)

112

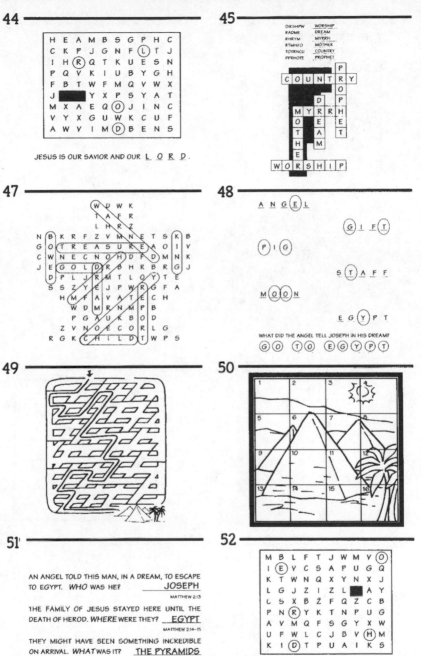

44

JESUS IS OUR SAVIOR AND OUR L O R D .

45

OIRSHPW — WORSHIP
RADME — DREAM
RHRYM — MYRRH
RTMHFO — MOTHER
TOYRNCU — COUNTRY
FPRHOTE — PROPHET

47

48

A N G E L

G I F T

P I G

S T A F F

M O O N

E G Y P T

WHAT DID THE ANGEL TELL JOSEPH IN HIS DREAM?
G O   T O   E G Y P T

49

50

51

AN ANGEL TOLD THIS MAN, IN A DREAM, TO ESCAPE
TO EGYPT. *WHO* WAS HE?   **JOSEPH**

MATTHEW 2:13

THE FAMILY OF JESUS STAYED HERE UNTIL THE
DEATH OF HEROD. *WHERE* WERE THEY?   **EGYPT**

MATTHEW 2:14–15

THEY MIGHT HAVE SEEN SOMETHING INCREDIBLE
ON ARRIVAL. *WHAT* WAS IT?   **THE PYRAMIDS**

52

AFTER THE DEATH OF H E R O D , THE
FAMILY OF JESUS RETURNED TO NAZARETH.

53

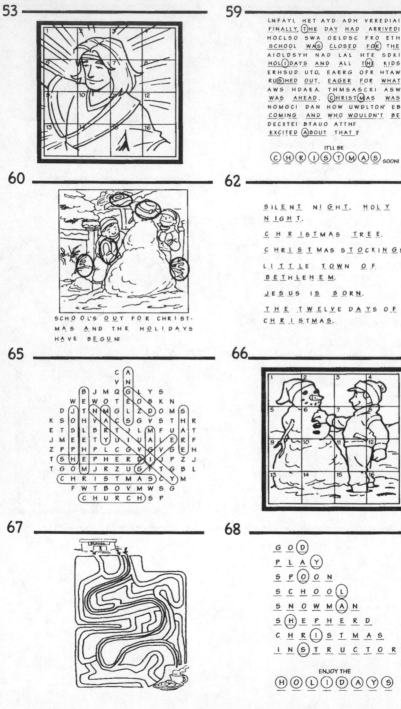

59

LNFAYL HET AYD ADH VRREDIAI
FINALLY, THE DAY HAD ARRIVED!
HOCLSO SWA OELDSC FRO ETH
SCHOOL WAS CLOSED FOR THE
AIOLDSYH NAD LAL HTE SDKI
HOLIDAYS AND ALL THE KIDS
ERHSUD UTO. EAERG OFR HTAW
RUSHED OUT. EAGER FOR WHAT
AWS HDAEA. THMSASCRI ASW
WAS AHEAD. CHRISTMAS WAS
NOMGCI DAN HOW UWDLTON' EB
COMING AND WHO WOULDN'T BE
DECXTEI BTAUO ATTH?
EXCITED ABOUT THAT?

IT'LL BE
C H R I S T M A S SOON!

60

SCHOOL'S OUT FOR CHRIST-
MAS AND THE HOLIDAYS
HAVE BEGUN!

62

SILENT NIGHT. HOLY
NIGHT.

CHRISTMAS TREE.

CHRISTMAS STOCKINGS.

LITTLE TOWN OF
BETHLEHEM.

JESUS IS BORN.

THE TWELVE DAYS OF
CHRISTMAS.

65

66

67

68

G O D
P L A Y
S P O O N
S C H O O L
S N O W M A N
S H E P H E R D
C H R I S T M A S
I N S T R U C T O R

ENJOY THE
H O L I D A Y S

69

THIS MAN HAS A LOT TO TEACH YOU IF YOU SHOW UP ONCE A WEEK. *WHO* IS HE? PASTOR

HE'LL SHOW YOU HOW TO GET DOWN THE MOUNTAIN SAFELY. *WHO* IS HE? SKI INSTRUCTOR

IT DOESN'T FLY AND IT MAKES YOUR MOUTH WATER EVERY YEAR. *WHAT* IS IT? TURKEY

IT IS VERY DIFFICULT WAITING TO FIND OUT THE CONTENTS OF THIS. *WHAT* IS IT? GIFT

AT THIS TIME OF YEAR, YOU'RE THINKING OF WHAT IS AHEAD. *WHERE* ARE YOU? SCHOOL

70

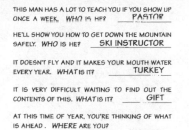

SNOWBALL FIGHTS ARE A LOT OF FUN, BUT TRY NOT TO H U R T ANYONE!

72

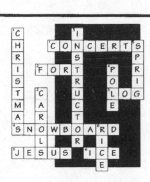

73

ERTE — TREE
KURTYE — TURKEY
ENRTANSOM — ORNAMENTS
NSRTEPT — PRESENT
HHBETELME — BETHLEHEM
IANSGTK — SKATING

74

1. BEGINS THE WORD *NUT* AND ENDS THE WORD *MOON*. N
2. APPEARS ONCE IN *ICE* AND TWICE IN *SKIIS*. I
3. THIS LETTER IS FOUND IN *BEGAN* BUT NOT IN *BEGUN*. A
4. APPEARS TWICE IN *BOOT* BUT ONLY ONCE IN *POLE*. O
5. FOUND TWICE IN BOTH *SNOWSHOE* AND *SOCKS*. S
6. YOU'LL FIND THIS IN *LESS* BUT NOT IN *LOSS*. E
7. BEGINS *TREE* AND IS IN THE MIDDLE OF *MOTOR*. T
8. APPEARS ONCE IN *SISTER* AND TWICE IN *BROTHER*. R

YOU WILL BE WITH CHILD AND GIVE BIRTH TO A SON, AND YOU ARE TO GIVE HIM THE NAME JESUS

75

SNOW	R A I N
UP	D O W N
RECEIVE	G I V E
DARK	L I G H T
FULL	E M P T Y
HAPPY	S A D
SISTER	B R O T H E R

CHRIST, THE TRUE M E A N I N G OF CHRISTMAS.

76

ON NLBAOLWS GTIHF SI EOPMLETC
NO SNOWBALL FIGHT IS COMPLETE

HTUTOIW A NRFWOOTS OT RERTATE
WITHOUT A SNOW FORT TO RETREAT

OT DAN EIHD NL KMAE SA YANM
TO AND HIDE IN. MAKE AS MANY

OSWN CRRISO SA UENEDE DAN
SNOW BRICKS AS NEEDED AND

TCAKS HMTE NO AHEC ORHET, KIGANM
STACK THEM ON EACH OTHER, MAKING

SREU HET IINSOJ REA GGDTSRKAE.
SURE THE JOINTS ARE STAGGERED.

U'YLOL EB BVNCEIINLI
YOU'LL BE INVINCIBLE!

YOU'LL NEED A

S N O W F O R T

80

THE THREE WISE MEN.

TURKEY WITH ALL THE TRIMMINGS.

CHRIST, THE SAVIOR, IS BORN.

IT'S BETTER TO GIVE THAN TO RECEIVE.

CHRISTMAS EVE.

MERRY CHRISTMAS AND A HAPPY NEW YEAR!

81

T O B O G G A N
S N O W F O R T
S N O W M O B I L E
I C E F I S H I N G
D R U M
S N O W M A N

WHAT'S REALLY, REALLY BIG AND COVERED WITH SNOW?

M O U N T A I N

82

SKIS HELP GET YOU QUICKLY FROM THE TOP TO THE BOTTOM. *WHERE* ARE YOU? _____ MOUNTAIN

THIS PERSON RECEIVED A MIRACLE AND THE SAVIOR WAS BORN. *WHO* WAS IT? _____ MARY

THREE MEN FROM THE EAST VISITED THIS SMALL TOWN. *WHERE* WERE THEY? _____ BETHLEHEM

IT IS MADE WAY UP NORTH, BUT YOU CAN MAKE ONE TOO. *WHAT* IS IT? _____ IGLOO

WITH THIS AND A HORSE YOU CAN GO ANYWHERE IN THE SNOW. *WHAT* IS IT? _____ SLEIGH

ON THIS, YOU ENJOY THE SAME SPORT IN WINTER AND SUMMER. *WHAT* ARE THEY? _____ SKIS

83

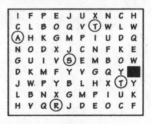

84

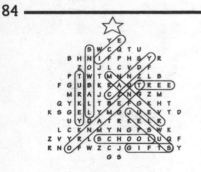

85

CHRISTMAS IS A TIME TO S T A R T
THINKING ABOUT OTHERS!

86

S K I
G I V E
I G L O O
D I N N E R
P R E S E N T
H O L I D A Y S
B E T H L E H E M

"TO YOU, A S A V I O R IS BORN."

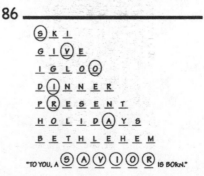

S N O W S H O E S

(crossword grid with GLOVES, SNOWMOBILE, SNOWMAN, BASKET, SKIS)

YVNREOEE ELVOS ICVEGERIN
EVERYONE <u>LOVES</u> RE<u>C</u>E<u>I</u>VING
FTIGS TA MRAHCTSS! NDA MEOS
GIFTS AT CHR<u>IST</u>MAS <u>AND</u> <u>SO</u>ME
VEHA NVEE ROSEEDYCDI HET OYJ
HAVE EV<u>E</u>N D<u>I</u>SCOVERED THE JOY
AHTT MESCO NI NIIGVG SGFTI.
THAT COME<u>S</u> IN GIVING GIFTS.
IHT6 TUGMOC 5I EA5UB NO
TH<u>I</u>S CUSTOM <u>I</u>S BA5E<u>D</u> ON
GTF15 GOBRUTH OT HTE OWBENRN
GIFTS BROUGHT TO THE NE<u>W</u>BORN
EU5J5. <u>JESUS</u>.

Ⓦ Ⓘ Ⓢ Ⓔ Ⓜ Ⓔ Ⓝ OR MAGI,
KINGS FROM THE EAST, CARRIED GIFTS FOR THE LORD.

SICK	H E A L T H Y
RUN	W A L K
BUY	S E L L
UNWRAP	W R A P
TEACH	L E A R N
FAST	S L O W
SHRINK	G R O W
LAST	F I R S T

A PLACE OF REFUGE:
Ⓢ N Ⓞ W Ⓕ Ⓞ R T

B H Q I P C K R D S
S J N U D L N F I A
D W A S X Y U W T N
M P K G H B S M E K
Q   F X C J P Y C X
C Q N Y T G H W Q
G U M X F W A R J B
R A T J U I P Y V R
M O I G H B T D F K

JESUS WAS BORN BECAUSE OF GOD'S LOVE FOR
YOU! IN HIM, YOU TOO CAN L O V E OTHERS.

T H E   L I T T L E   D R U M M E R
B O Y.

S T A R   O F   B E T H L E H E M.

P E A C E   O N   E A R T H   A N D
G O O D W I L L   T O   M E N.

A   B A B Y   L Y I N G   I N   A
M A N G E R

W H I T E   C H R I S T M A S.

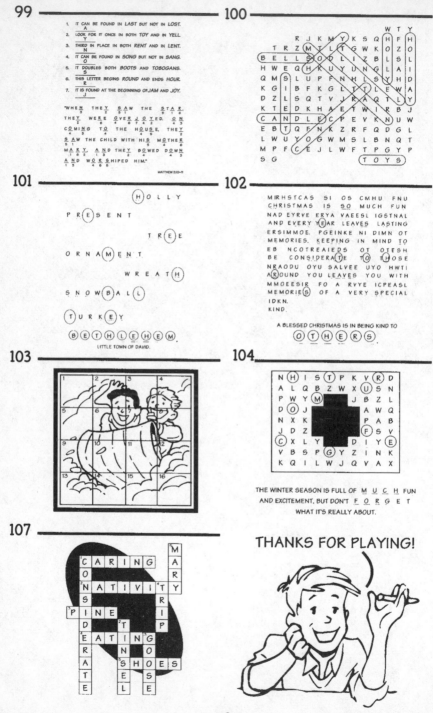

99

1. IT CAN BE FOUND IN LAST BUT NOT IN LOST. — A
2. LOOK FOR IT ONCE IN BOTH TOY AND IN YELL. — Y
3. THIRD IN PLACE IN BOTH RENT AND IN LENT. — N
4. IT CAN BE FOUND IN SONG BUT NOT IN SANG. — O
5. IT DOUBLES BOTH BOOTS AND TOBOGANS. — S
6. THIS LETTER BEGINS ROUND AND ENDS HOUR. — R
7. IT IS FOUND AT THE BEGINNING OF JAM AND JOY. — J

"WHEN THEY SAW THE STAR, THEY WERE OVERJOYED. ON COMING TO THE HOUSE, THEY SAW THE CHILD WITH HIS MOTHER MARY, AND THEY BOWED DOWN AND WORSHIPED HIM."

MATTHEW 2:10-11

100

Word search grid with found words: BELL, CANDLE, TOYS, NOODLE, etc.

101

(H)OLLY
PR(E)SENT
TR(E)E
ORNA(M)ENT
WREAT(H)
SNOW(B)ALL
(T)URK(E)Y
(B)ET(H)L(E)H(E)M

LITTLE TOWN OF DAVID.

102

MIRHSTCAS SI OS CMHU FNU
CHRISTMAS IS SO MUCH FUN
NAD EYRVE ERYA VAEESL IGSTNAL
AND EVERY YEAR LEAVES LASTING
ERSIMMOE. PGEINKE NI DIMN OT
MEMORIES. KEEPING IN MIND TO
EB NCOTREAIEDS OT OTESH
BE CONSIDERATE TO THOSE
NRAODU OYU SALVEE UYO HWTI
AROUND YOU LEAVES YOU WITH
MMOEESIR FO A RVYE ICPEASL
MEMORIES OF A VERY SPECIAL
IDKN.
KIND.

A BLESSED CHRISTMAS IS IN BEING KIND TO
(O)T(H)(E)(R)(S)

103

104

THE WINTER SEASON IS FULL OF M U C H FUN
AND EXCITEMENT, BUT DON'T F O R G E T
WHAT IT'S REALLY ABOUT.

107

Crossword grid:
CARING, NATIVITY, PINE, EATING, SHOES, MARY, CONSIDERATE, TRIP, TINSEL, NOSE, CRATE, etc.

THANKS FOR PLAYING!

Check out these bonus pages from
DARE YOU NOT TO LAUGH!

Available from Barbour Publishing, Inc.

INTRODUCTION:
DARE YOU NOT TO LAUGH!

Worried mom: My son thinks he's a dog. He barks at people and chases cats.

Doctor: Hmm. . . . How long has he behaved like this?

Mom: Since he was a puppy.

Did you know that the Bible says "a cheerful heart is good medicine" (Proverbs 17:22)? Well, here's a healthy dose for kids ages eight to twelve.

Dare You Not to Laugh: Great Clean Jokes for Kids is jam-packed with jokes on school and church, sports and the outdoors, family and food, technology and transportation, you name it.

They're clean! They're funny! We dare you not to laugh! We Double Dog Dare you—even Triple Dog Dare you—on some of them!

1.
SCRIPTURAL SNICKERS

How many animals did Moses take on the ark?

Moses didn't take any animals on the ark. Noah did.

Why didn't Noah fish much?

He only had two worms.

What did the well-mannered sheep say to the other animals waiting to get on the ark?

"After ewe!"

What did Noah say to the frogs?

"Hop on in!"

Who spent most of their time on their knees in the ark?

The birds of pray.

After the flood, why didn't some of the snakes "go forth and multiply"?

They couldn't—they were adders.

What was Noah's profession?

He was an ark-itect.

Was Noah the first out of the ark?

No, he came forth out of the ark.

What did Noah say as he was loading the ark?

"Now I herd everything."

Why didn't anyone play cards on the ark?

Because Noah sat on the deck.

Which animals did Noah distrust?

The cheetahs.

What kind of light did Noah have on the ark?

Floodlights.

Which animals were the last to leave the ark?

The elephants. It took time for them to pack their trunks.

DOUBLE DOG DARE

What kind of man was Boaz before he married?

Ruthless.

How did Jonah feel when the whale swallowed him?

Down in the mouth.

How long did Cain dislike his brother?

As long as he was Abel.

Who was the first tennis player in the Bible?

Joseph—he served in Pharaoh's court.

Who was the fastest runner in history?
Adam. He was first in the human
race.

Who was the shortest man in the Bible?
Knee-high-miah (Nehemiah).

What season was it when Eve ate the
fruit?
Early in the fall.

DOUBLE DOG DARE

Which Bible character had
no parents?
Joshua. He was the son
of Nun.

What do people today have that Adam
didn't?
Ancestors.

What time of day was Adam created?
   Just a little before Eve.

What's the first court case mentioned
in the Bible?
   Joshua Judges Ruth.

TRIPLE DOG DARE

Which part of Israel was
especially wealthy?
   The Jordan River.
   The banks were always
   overflowing.

When is baseball first mentioned in the
Bible?
   Genesis 1:1—"In the big inning. . ."

What was the first medication in the
Bible?
   When God gave Moses two tablets.

Why didn't Samson want to argue with Delilah?

He didn't want to split hairs.

How do we know Peter was a wealthy fisherman?

Because of his net income.

Where was Solomon's temple located?

On the side of his head.

TRIPLE DOG DARE

Who was the most intelligent man in the Bible?
Abraham, because he knew a Lot.